THE RANCH.

NCH VERSES

LONDON

RANCH VERSES

BY

WILLIAM LAWRENCE CHITTENDEN

G. P. PUTNAM'S SONS

NEW YORK   LONDON
27 WEST TWENTY-THIRD STREET   24 BEDFORD STREET, STRAND

The Knickerbocker Press

1893

Electrotyped, Printed, and Bound by
The Knickerbocker Press, New York
G. P. Putnam's Sons

THE verses in this little volume are offsprings of solitude—born in idle hours on a Texas ranch.

W. L. C.

CHITTENDEN'S RANCH,
ANSON, TEXAS,
January, 1893.

CONTENTS.

v

Bah!

d bless em!
d bless em!

Contents.

ix

ILLUSTRATIONS.

* Reproduced from an illustration by Mr. Harry Fenn, in *Picturesque America*, published by Messrs. D. Appleton & Co.

RANCH VERSES.

HIDDEN.

TO GEN. R. M. GANO.

A FAR on the pathless prairies
  The rarest of flowers abound ;
And in the dark caves of the valleys
  There is wealth that will never be found ;
So there are sweet songs in the silence
  That never will melt into sound.

The twilight illumines her banners
  With colors no artist can teach ;
And aloft in the sky there are sermons
  Too mighty for mortals to preach ;
So life has its lovely ideals
  Too lofty for language to reach.

Afar on the sea there 's a music
  That the shore never knows in its rest ;
And in the green depths of the forest
  There are choirs that carol unblest ;
So, deep in the heart there 's a music
  And a cadence that 's never expressed.

MY OLD FRIEND, "THE MAJAH GREEN."

IN the sunny land of Texas, where Tom Ochil-
tree's at home,
Where the cowman swings the lasso and the wild
jack-rabbits roam ;
Where hearts of gallant gentlemen are full of sand
and glow,
And the prairies laugh to plenty with the tickle of
the hoe ;
Where the vote is always solid—on the democratic
side,
And old "Tariff Mills" is grinding grist and
thought from far and wide ;
Where the mocking-birds are singing on the
feathery mesquite trees,
And the zephyrs soft are flinging rarest fragrance
to the breeze ;
Where the rustlers from the ranches chase the
wild-eyed maverick steer,
And the pitching pony prances o'er the dog-towns
far and near ;
Where the antelope is grazing, thirty miles from
Abilene,
There it was I met the "Majah"—my old friend,
"The Majah Green."

. . . .

He had led the Southern armies, when their
banners floated free,

From the winding Rappahannock to the tropic
   Mexique Sea.
Ay, he told me wondrous stories of the days
   "befo' de wah,"
When he "owned the pertest darkies," "that was
   raised in Georgah, sah."
And he spoke about his boyhood in a "rah old
   Southern town,"
On the lazy Ocmulgee, with its houses old and
   brown ;
Where they raised big sweet potatoes, and the
   "little goober vines,"
And the "roses blushed forever," 'neath the softly
   wooing pines.
But at last he came to Texas, to the "woolly
   wild " frontier,
Where he "founded Anson City," in the spring-
   time of the year.
There he built his "little homestead," garlanded
   with eglantine,
Where the hollyhocks threw kisses to the fragrant
   jessamine.
He was bluff and stout and hearty, rather pompous
   in his mien,
Yet he had a kindly "howdy" for all, had Major
   Green.

   .   .   .   .

Perhaps he was not educated, as a tenderfoot
   conceives,
But he *scanned the books of nature*, as the seasons
   turned the leaves.

He was very fond of hunting—that's the reason
    he liked me ;
Many a time we roamed together o'er the prairies
    broad and free,
Where the Double Mountains standeth, and will
    stand for many a day,
Till the *Seventh Trumpet* soundeth, and the earth
    shall pass away.
Oft we watched the gilded banners of the golden
    hours depart,
When the twilight's richest beauty sheds its
    shadows o'er the heart.
Soon the evening fire was kindled, and we rested
    on the ground,
While the breathing stars shed lustre o'er the
    wilderness profound.
Then the Major told his stories, sang some deep
    bass roundelay
To his " Lily of the Valley," or " Old Dixie," far
    away.
Yes, his heart beat high but kindly, square and
    honest, nothing mean
'Bout that " Vetran, sah," "the Majah," my old
    friend, the Major Green.

.   .   .   .

Hark ! the lonely doves are cooing, in the weeping
    mesquite vale,
And the south winds sad are sighing o'er the old
    McKenzie trail ;
Ah, they miss that sturdy figure, for his honest feet
    have trod

Far beyond the sunset mountains where his spirit
    went to God.
The prairie flowers are waving o'er a lonely little
    mound,
For the Major roams the borders of the Happy
    Hunting Ground.
He has crossed the Royal River that rolls on to
    crystal seas,
And has found his old commander, Stonewall
    Jackson, " 'neath the trees."
They are resting from their labors ; oh, I know
    that smile serene
That in olden days illumined my old friend, " The
    Majah Green."

WHY NOT BE HAPPY TO-DAY?

I HAVE questioned my hopes of the future,
   I have doubted my dreams of the past,
I have roamed through the realms of ambition,
With visions too lovely to last.
I have longed for youth's fondest ideals,
But those phantoms are now far away,
And at last fair philosophy whispers,
Oh, why not be happy to-day?

Though storm clouds may darken life's valley,
(And each heart has some shadows of care,)
The bright sun will soon gild the heavens,
And thy troubles will melt into air.

So what is the use of repining ?
Will it bless or ennoble you, pray ?
No !—The world does not care for your whining,
So why not be happy to-day ?

Ah, the old world at heart is too solemn,
For life is at best full of trials ;
But try to be cheerful, 't will help you,
If you brighten all pathways with smiles.
Then life will be well worth the living,
Let kindness illumine its way,
And with Hope's gilded banners before us
Let 's strive to be happy to-day.

———

SUB ROSA.

I HAVE heard the robins singing
    Where the sweet magnolia grows ;
I have seen the zephyrs flinging
    Twilight kisses to the rose ;
But a sweeter song has filled me
    Than the birds in perfumed bowers,
And a softer kiss has thrilled me
    Than the south winds on the flowers.

I have felt the lilies blowing
    Dewy fragrance in the morn ;
I have seen the sunbeams glowing
    Golden blushes on the corn ;

But I know a flower that 's fairer
  Than the lilies ever grew,
And I love a blush that 's rarer
  Than the sunbeam's softest hue.

I have seen the moonbeams flying
  Over starlit, silvery seas ;
I have heard the zephyrs sighing
  Through the orange blossomed trees ;
But a purer ray has blessed me
  Than the moonlight on the sands,
And a softer sigh caressed me
  Than the breath of tropic lands.

She is fairer than the flowers ;
  She is sweeter than the rose ;
And her heart of kindness showers
  Blessings everywhere she goes.
Altruistic—without sinning—
  She 's an angel from the sky,
(Far above my earthly winning)—
  She 's *engaged!* and so am I !

———

TO THE MOCKING-BIRD.

A FAR from noisy, tuneless throngs,
  Which worship round the cities' shrine,
I listen to thy moonlight songs,
  Thy melodies divine.

I drink the sweetness of thy lay
Where fragrant breezes softly play
Through silvery banners of whispering moss
Which wave beneath the Southern Cross.

I hear thy clear and restful note
   Upon the evening air arise,
Until the silence seems to float
   With music from the skies.
Yes, I have listened till I felt
My restless heart begin to melt,
Until my spirit longed to be
In tuneful harmony with thee.

Ah, there 's an echo in thy strain
   Which soothes the tired, troubled breast,
And bids life's passions sleep again
   And charms the soul to rest.
But who, indeed, can truly pay
Just tribute to thy heavenly lay ?
Not I, alas ! No words of mine
Can echo those rare songs of thine.

––––––––

THE RANCHMAN'S STORY.

I LONG had lived a lonely life
   Far from the world apart.
A dweller 'midst a land of dreams,
   Close, close to Nature's heart.

Ah, Nature always speaks the truth !
  (In her I still believe)
And so I passed my earnest youth
  Unpractised to deceive.

I loved mankind—my hopes were high,
  For I had often trod
Upon the lofty mountain heights
  Whose summits point to God !
My heart was tuned by songs of birds,
  My life was free from care ;
I dwelt in youth's rare palaces,
  'Midst castles in the air.

At last I left my prairie home,
  I roamed to distant strands,
And lived in courtly marble halls
  In stately Northern lands.
Ah ! there I met a queen of art,
  A lovely woman dear,
"An idol for a poet's heart,"
  My "Lady Vere de Vere !"

Yes, she was young and proud and fair—
  Fair as the evening star—
So, "poet-like," I idealized
  And worshipped her afar.
Ah, yes, I loved her high-bred mien,
  She seemed so pure and kind !
She praised my songs, she heard my words—
  Oh, why was I so blind ?

To ardent speech and Southern hearts
　She said she was unused ;
Oh, yes, she " liked an earnest man " ;
　She "loved to be amused ! "
And so I lost my foolish heart ;
　She kept it for a day,
Till Fate decreed that we should part
　And strand me far away.

Last week a scented letter came
　My visions to dispel ;
It brought her dainty wedding-cards
　And that long word—" Farewell ! "
To-day my lady will be wed,
　To-day the bells will ring,
And yet the world seems cold and dead,
　My birds have ceased to sing.

To-day alone, in lonely lands,
　Where Bridesmaid Nature smiles,
I hear a muffled wedding march
　In dim cathedral aisles,
'Midst all the throngs of beauty there,
　Of all that pomp and pride,
I only see the rippling hair,
　The pure eyes of the bride !

The proud procession sweeps along
　Behind her blossomed veil ;
It pauses there in silence now
　Beside the chancel rail.

The words are said—her answer comes
  (My dream was false and fleet)—
But still I strew my blessings there
  Around her dainty feet.

Ah ! now there is no peace for me,
  I roam life's plains alone,
'Midst fervent hopes of former days
  With wrecks of ruin strown.
Oh, how the mournful zephyrs sigh
  Her last words in my ear !
My world, my heart, my life is full
  Of Lady Vere de Vere !

Though I can tame the wild mustang
  And breast the ocean's ire,
And face the Norther's freezing blast
  Or check the prairie fire,
I cannot curb a restless heart,
  Nor stem Love's swelling tide ;
'T was wealth that burned our souls apart—
  " Farewell ! " pale victim bride !

A SONNET—THE PRAIRIES.

I LOVE the prairies broad and free,
  For there I know and there I feel
  My heart is not a thing of steel.
Lost in this tawny, fragrant sea

I breathe and hear that minstrelsy
  Which Nature's vibrant chords reveal,
  And Nature's tuneful songs appeal
To all that 's best and good in me.
  The stars, the clouds, the azure skies
And viewless vastness all combine
    To broaden life ; yes, here my spirit soars
      and flies
Beyond the world's low level line
  Till, lost, forgetful of life's sighs,
It dwells in miraged realms divine.

––––––

THE COWBOYS' CHRISTMAS BALL.

TO THE RANCHMEN OF TEXAS.

'WAY out in Western Texas, where the Clear
    Fork's waters flow,
Where the cattle are "a-browzin'," an' the Spanish
    ponies grow ;
Where the Northers "come a-whistlin'" from
    beyond the Neutral strip ;
And the prairie dogs are sneezin', as if they had
    "The Grip" ;
Where the cayotes come a-howlin' 'round the
    ranches after dark,
And the mocking-birds are singin' to the lovely
    "medder lark" ;
Where the 'possum and the badger, and rattle-
    snakes abound,

And the monstrous stars are winkin' o'er a wil-
    derness profound ;
Where lonesome, tawny prairies melt into airy
    streams,
While the Double Mountains slumber, in heavenly
    kinds of dreams ;
Where the antelope is grazin' and the lonely
    plovers call—
It was there that I attended "The Cowboys'
    Christmas Ball."

The town was Anson City, old Jones's county
    seat,
Where they raise Polled Angus cattle, and waving
    whiskered wheat ;
Where the air is soft and "bammy," an' dry an'
    full of health,
And the prairies is explodin' with agricultural
    wealth ;
Where they print the *Texas Western*, that Hec.
    McCann supplies,
With news and yarns and stories, uv most amazin'
    size ;
Where Frank Smith "pulls the badger," on know-
    in' tenderfeet,
And Democracy 's triumphant, and mighty hard
    to beat ;
Where lives that good old hunter, John Milsap
    from Lamar,
Who "used to be the Sheriff, back East, in Paris,
    sah ! "

'T was there, I say, at Anson, with the lively " wid-
　　der Wall,"
That I went to that reception, " The Cowboys'
　　Christmas Ball."

The boys had left the ranches and come to town
　　in piles ;
The ladies—" kinder scatterin' "—had gathered in
　　for miles.
And yet the place was crowded, as I remember
　　well,
'T was got for the occasion, at " The Morning Star
　　Hotel."
The music was a fiddle an' a lively tambourine,
And a " viol come imported," by the stage from
　　Abilene.
The room was togged out gorgeous—with mistle-
　　toe and shawls,
And candles flickered frescoes, around the airy
　　walls.
The " wimmin folks" looked lovely—the boys
　　looked kinder treed,
Till their leader commenced yellin': " Whoa !
　　fellers, let 's stampede,"
And the music started sighin', an' awailin' through
　　the hall,
As a kind of introduction to " The Cowboys'
　　Christmas Ball."

The leader was a feller that came from Swenson's
　　Ranch,

"THEY CALLED HIM WINDY BILLY."

They called him "Windy Billy," from "little
    Deadman's Branch."
His rig was "kinder keerless," big spurs and high-
    heeled boots ;
He had the reputation that comes when "fellers
    shoots."
His voice was like a bugle upon the mountain's
    height ;
His feet were animated, an' a *mighty, movin' sight,*
When he commenced to holler, "Neow fellers,
    stake yer pen !
"Lock horns ter all them heifers, an' russle 'em
    like men.
"Saloot yer lovely critters ; neow swing an' let
    'em go,
"Climb the grape vine 'round 'em—all hands do-
    ce-do !
"You Mavericks, jine the round-up—Jest skip her
    waterfall,"
Huh ! hit wuz gettin' active, "The Cowboys'
    Christmas Ball ! "

The boys were tolerable skittish, the ladies power-
    ful neat,
That old bass viol's music *just got there with both
    feet !*
That wailin', frisky fiddle, I never shall forget ;
And Windy kept a singin'—I think I hear him
    yet—
"O Xes, chase your squirrels, an' cut 'em to one
    side,

"Spur Treadwell to the centre, with Cross P Charley's bride,

"Doc. Hollis down the middle, an' twine the ladies' chain,

"Varn Andrews pen the fillies in big T Diamond's train.

"All pull yer freight tergether, neow swallow fork an' change,

"'Big Boston' lead the trail herd, through little Pitchfork's range.

"Purr 'round yer gentle pussies, neow rope 'em! Balance all!"

Huh! hit wuz gettin' active—"The Cowboys' Christmas Ball!"

The dust riz fast an' furious, we all just galloped 'round,

Till the scenery got so giddy, that Z Bar Dick was downed.

We buckled to our partners, an' told 'em to hold on,

Then shook our hoofs like lightning, until the early dawn.

Don't tell me 'bout cotillions, or germans. No sir 'ee!

That whirl at Anson City just takes the cake with me.

I 'm sick of lazy shufflin's, of them I 've had my fill,

Give me a frontier break-down, backed up by Windy Bill.

McAllister ain't nowhar ! when Windy leads the
    show,
I 've seen 'em both in harness, and so I sorter
    know—
Oh, Bill, I sha'n't forget yer, and I 'll oftentimes
    recall,
That lively gaited sworray — " The Cowboys'
    Christmas Ball."

MONTCLAIR.

DEAR lovely mountain town, farewell,
    Though we, alas, must part,
Thy landscape beauties long shall dwell
    Like memories in my heart.

As some lone river onward flows
    To seek a restful sea,
So shall my spirit seek repose
    In restful dreams of thee.

Though far in distant lands I roam,
    A haunted wanderer there,
I 'll think of thee, my boyhood's home,
    Cool mountain-browed Montclair.

I love thy crags and purple hills,
    Thy views of distant seas,
Thy fruitful vines and whispering rills,
    Thy groves of murmuring trees.

2

How oft I trod thy woodland vales,
   Along thy shaded streams,
A hunter lost 'midst gameless dales,
   In boyhood's land of dreams.

Though Time may blight life's youthful hopes,
   Fond Memory's fancies fair
Shall twine rich garlands round thy slopes,
   Proud mountain town, Montclair !

THE DIFFERENCE.

TEN years ago, my lovely Kate,
   Eighteen was I with you,
But now when I am twenty-eight
   You 're only twenty-two !

How is it in Time's equal race
   My years have yours surpassed ?
" Because," laughed Kate, with roguish face,
   " Because you *lived so fast!* "

GALVESTON.

TO " M. P. W."

WHERE sea-gulls fair are flying
   Above a lonely sea,
And zephyrs rare are sighing
   Across the sandy lea ;

Where oleanders blossom beneath a generous sun,
There by the sobbing billows, dreams lovely Gal-
 veston.

  Her roses bloom forever
   Beneath an azure sky.
  Her sunlight fadeth never,
   For summer lingers nigh.
There at the gates of Texas, in tropic garlands
 drest,
She smiles in budding beauty—the queen of the
 Southwest.

WHEN THE NORTHER SIGHS.

RONDEAU.

WHEN the Norther sighs, and the storm winds
  pour
From the cold, bleak coasts of Labrador,
How pleasant then, by the big log fire,
To watch the cheerful flames leap higher
And hear the great wide chimneys roar.
  What hidden realms can the mind explore
  In the mystic lands of classic lore?
  To what bold flights may the Muse aspire
   When the Norther sighs?

Then here afar, when the wild winds war,
And the cayote howls at my lonely door, .

I love to wake the slumbering lyre,
For my spirit soars beyond care's pyre,
And I dream old dreams, beloved of yore,
    When the Norther sighs.

"IN HIS NAME."

TO MRS. MARGARET BOTTOME.

IN fair Virginia's Lotus Land, where sings the
    whippoorwill,
And slumb'rous sunlight loves to woo the rippling
    mountain rill,
Long years ago a careless lad, fresh freed from
    droning school,
I roamed fair Shenandoah's vales, in meadows rich
    and cool.
I saw the river sweep along through fields of wav-
    ing grain ;
I heard the piping bobolinks sing olden songs
    again ;
And high upon the Blue Ridge heights, where
    rarest zephyrs dwell,
I wandered on 'midst sylvan scenes into a lonely
    dell,
Where, hidden in the weeping grass, beyond all
    strife or blame,
I found a slab which simply said, " Erected in His
    Name."

I scanned that slanting little cross and paused
    beside the mound,
To read the story buried there, but nothing more
    was found.
I knew some soldier, tired and worn, from earthly
    battles free,
Had answered to his last tattoo and Death's grim
    reveille.
Yet who he was or whence he came, alas ! no one
    can tell
The weeping mother of that son just where her
    hero fell.
Perhaps some mournful maiden now is sighing for
    the tread
That 's crossed the purple twilight hills to cities of
    the dead.
Perhaps some prattling children long for steps that
    never came,
And lilies of the valley bloom and blossom " In
    His Name."

Some aged father's manly prop and loving sister's
    care
Has crossed to twilight realms of rest in valleys
    over there.
The sunlight now is smiling soft upon that lonely
    lea,
The silvery Shenandoah sweeps her blossoms to
    the sea ;
Yet unforgotten sorrow broods around that pensive
    scene,

And weeping seasons shed their woes upon the
 misty green.
The hooing owls murmur low, and sad the whip-
 poorwills
Echo the story of that mound o'er old Virginia's
 hills ;
But when at last fair glory calls for all her sons of
 fame,
The silent watcher over all will answer, " In His
 Name."

THE RANCHMAN'S LETTER.

AT a lonely old ranch by the fire to-night,
 At my ranch on the Texas frontier,
Old memories, my lady, now prompt me to write
 To a friend who is distant—yet near.

While the fire dreams on in its warm chimney bed
 And the owls are calling " Tu Whoo ! "
Alone I recall the fond past that is fled,
 Alone I am thinking of you.

And you ? as you flirt with some gay millionaire,
 Or among " the four hundred " seek rest,
Do you ever remember, my proud Lady Clare,
 Your friend in " the wild, woolly West " ?

Have you then forgotten our joys of the past,
  That parting, and silent good-bye ?
Alas, those bright days were too lovely to last
  For such a poor fellow as I.

The parts that we play on the broad stage of life
  Are now very different, I fear ;
For while you are leading 'midst fashionable strife
  I chase the shy " maverick steer."

You dwell in proud mansions on Fifth Avenue,
  Sometimes you are seen at Long Branch ;
I live here alone with a cowboy or two
  'Midst the *woes* of a *bachelor's ranch.*

You dine on rare viands and costly champagne,
  You lunch with Delmonico's queens,
In the summer you live in the hotels of Maine ;
  I live on *boiled bacon and beans.*

You drive in proud state, your coachman is dark,
  You pose in your carriage, of course ;
You travel in Pullmans to Tuxedo Park,
  I ride on a wild pitching horse !

Your dresses are poems ! your bills are immense !
  At least I imagine they are ;
They make a fine figure—in dollars and cents ;
  They are paid by your frowning papa.

You go to receptions and Patriarchs' balls,
　You gossip at five o'clock teas,
You 're a slave to gay fashion !　Oh, how it
　　　enthralls ;
　I call it a farce, if you please.

Yes !　yes !　it 's a sham !　You are wasting your
　　life
　In those fashionable follies up there,—
You who would make such a lovable wife !
　I would court you myself—did I dare !

But alas, it can't be !　you would never live here,
　And prudence forbids me to speak ;
For while you are spending four thousand a year
　I subsist on two dollars a week !

———

MY MOTHER.

I KNOW a dear old lady
　Whose voice is soft and low,
Her face is like some picture,
　A dream of long ago.

She is not great nor famous,
　Nor known in realms of art,
But she is rich in treasures
　Which gild a kindly heart.

To see her is to bless her ;
    Her praise is on each tongue ;
She 's friends in all the aged,
    And " lovers in the young."

Her life 's a living sermon
    Of hope and gentle facts—
A text for human nature,
    That 's found in loving acts !

She fills her world with kindness,
    It brightens every spot.
She has her earthly sorrows,
    But yet of earth is not.

She 's patient, pure, and happy,
    In these her twilight days ;
Her lips are ever ready
    To comfort or to praise.

Her soul 's a gleam of sunshine,
    A rainbow in Life's showers ;
Her presence is a garden
    Of ever-blooming flowers,

Which Time can never wither,
    For recollections rare
Shall bloom around her memory,
    And twine Love's garlands there.

A BACHELOR'S DILEMMA.

M Y lady is lovely and noble and kind,
  Too noble for me, I am sure.
She 's the queen of all women, rich, true, and
  refined ;
  I am only gay-hearted and poor.

She 's a leader of fashion—has a home of her own ;
  Her mansions are wonderfully fair.
I am " only a poet "—I live all alone ;
  My castles are all in the air.

Alas, she 's too wealthy and stylish for me,
  Yet I love her far more than my life.
But I 'm too proud to marry—I never could be
  " A man that 's maintained by his wife."

" We were made for each other," of this I am sure;
  She likes me—I know by her eyes—
But alas, she 's so wealthy and I am so poor,
  I cannot support such a prize !

Then what in the world should a bachelor do
  Who is busted, teetotally, flat ?

  . . . . . .

Why ! I 'll ask for her hand, and her big *fortune*,
  too,
  Then—*work*—to *support her with that !*

A FARMER'S SONGS.

WAL, I reckon I 'm ole-fashioned, but them
    songs that Nacher sings
Iz the kind tu soothe my feelin's an' twang my ole
    heart strings.
When I sets back fer muzic, I expecks to hear sum
    chune
Thet will thrill through my ole buzzum like er
    robin's song in June.

Oh, I luv the brook's clear tinkle, fiddlin' onward
    to the sea
Ez it laughs aroun' the rushes whar the black-
    birds call " co chee " ;
Thar iz muzic uv a mornin' in the risin' songs uv
    birds,
More delightful tu my feelin's than the sweetest
    kind uv words.

Then at noon when I 'm er restin' 'neath the meller
    blossomed trees,
It iz sleepy-like an plezzant jes to hear the drowzy
    bees,
Or the lazy locus' hummin' on a peaceful summer
    day,
When the air iz warm an' fragrant with the clover
    tops an' hay.

Thar iz muzic tu at twilight, ez mos' every one
    allows,
In the chingle, changle, chingle, of the homeward
    windin' cows ;
An' when the chores iz finished ez the evenin'
    shadders falls,
I luv to hear the cattle *munchin' muzic in their*
    stalls.

An' at dusk when work is over, an' the air iz
    hushed an' still,
It is mournful-like an' plezzant jes to hear the
    whipperwill ;
Then at last when supper 's finished an' wife 's sot
    away the things,
Heow I dream an' loaf an' listen while the
    steamin' kettle sings.

When the winter storms cum' ragin', and the big
    log fires glow,
Heow I luv the chimbley's muzic, like a dirge from
    long ago ;
Yes, I reckon I 'm ole-fashioned, but the songs wot
    Nacher sings
Iz the kind tu soothe my feelin's an' twang my ole
    heart-strings.

TEXAS TYPES—THE COWBOY.

HE wears a big hat and big spurs and all that,
    And leggins of fancy fringed leather ;
He takes pride in his boots and the pistol he
    shoots,
    And he 's happy in all kinds of weather.

He is fond of his horse—'t is a bronco, of course,
    For, oh, he can ride like the Devil ;
He is old for his years, and he always appears
    To be foremost at round-up or revel.

He can sing, he can cook, yet his eyes have the
    look
    Of a man that to fear is a stranger ;
Yes, his cool, quiet nerve will always subserve
    In his wild life of duty and danger.

He gets little to eat and he guys tenderfeet,
    And for Fashion—oh, well, he 's " not in it ! "
He can rope a gay steer when he gets on his ear,
    At the rate of two-forty a minute !

His saddle 's the best in the wild, woolly West,
    Sometimes it will cost sixty dollars ;
Ah, he knows all the tricks, when he brands
    " Mavericks,"
    But his learning 's not gained from your scholars.

He is loyal as steel, but demands a square deal,
  And he hates and despises a coward.
Yet the cowboy you 'll find unto woman is kind,
  Though he 'll fight till by death overpowered.

Hence I say unto you, give the cowboy his due,
  And be kinder, my friends, toward his folly ;
For he 's generous and brave, though he may not
    behave
  Like your dudes, who are so melancholy.

A VILLAGE FABLE.

AS Death and the Devil were taking the air,
  In a beautiful village—the town of Montclair—
They came to a doctor, a true friend of both,
Who had *physicked himself*—and was dying forsooth !
" See here," wailed sad Death, " see here, Jolly Nick,
" Is our friend *Doctor B——* but alas, he 's quite sick:
" Yet his practice is large, as you 'll surely agree,
" For his patients keep coming to you and to me.
" Shall we spare him this time, at least for awhile ? "
" By all means ! " sang Nick, as he said, with a smile,
" Well, well, dearest Doctor, your call has been close;
" In the future *be careful, don't take your own dose,*
" But physic your patients, and *fire* them to me,
" And I with great *patience*, will at last *fire* thee ! "
" Ha, ha ! " laughed the Doctor, who relished all
    sport,
" 'T is truly a blessing to have friends at court."

KIND WORDS.

A KIND word now and then, my boys,
  A kind word here and there,
Will fill the weary world with joys
  And banish clouds of care ;
Though life may sometimes seem all wrong
  And heaven far away,
Don't lose your grip, just peg along,
  You 'll find that pluck will pay.

Don't be ashamed nor 'fraid, my boys,
  To show that you 've a heart,
Be bold and undismayed, my boys,
  But act a kindly part.
Don't wait until your friends are dead
  Their virtues to unfold,
Kind words in time, and timely said,
  Are worth their weight in gold.

Don't lean too much on prayers, my boys,
  Just find your text in acts ;
Be true, and fair, and square, my boys,
  Such preaching 's full of facts.
With kind words now and then, my boys,
  With kind words here and there,
Let 's fill the weary world with joys
  And banish clouds of care.

COULD I BUT FLY ON SEABIRD'S WING.

COULD I but fly on seabird's wing
   To Youth's green island realms of yore,
My restless spirit ne'er could cling
   To Manhood's dull and faded shore ;
But with a free, exultant flight
   I'd leave these chambered hours of care,
And wing my way to dreams of light,
   To dwell 'midst castles in the air.

Yes, there in Love's rare, rosy bowers
   I'd gather garlands bright with Hope,
Without one thought of wasted flowers
   Which withered on Ambition's slope.
Then might I trill some bugle song
   Which nations yet unborn would sing,
And Time might then my fame prolong,
   Could I but fly on seabird's wing.

THE PRODIGAL DAUGHTER.

IN the spring-time of youth, in life's early morn-
   ing,
When the blossoms were blowing from the old
   apple-trees,
And wistaria vines with their purple adorning

Were wooing the zephyrs and rich yellow bees,
The Prodigal came to the home of his leaving,
Where he played in the daisies a light-hearted
    boy,
And they welcomed him back, with the tears of
    receiving,
And twining affection and murmurs of joy.

.   .   .   .   .   .

When the cold winds of winter were sighing so
    dreary
Around the old house by the murmuring shore,
The Prodigal daughter, all tired and weary,
Crept back to the home of her girlhood once
    more ;
But they turned her away, o'er the moorland so
    lonely,
And the winds of despair moaned wild through her
    breast,
And death was her refuge, aye that, and that
    only,
For the Prodigal daughter, alas, has no rest !

THE LOVELY ROSALIE.

IN lively old New Jersey, where the laws are very
    blue,
And the applejack's the smoothest that a Texan
    ever knew ;
Where commuters roam in thousands and New
    Yorkers often flee

From the giddy cares of Gotham to the softly mur-
    muring sea ;
Where nobby Wall street brokers and Mugwumps
    often chat
'Bout the glories of "weak fishing" round the bars
    at Barnegat ;
Where they chase "imported beagles (?)" on the
    trail for anise-seed,
With that kindly English hunter, F. M. Wheeler,
    in the lead ;
Where the people are all "*culchawed,*" in that toney
    town Montclair,
Which is noted for its beauties and pure, salubrious
    air ;
Where abides the poet angler, known to fame as
    Dodge (H. C.),
It was there befell the wooing of the lovely
    Rosalie.

Her eyes were like twin violets, suffused in pearly
    dew,
Her cheeks bespoke the roses that twilight loves to
    woo ;
She seemed like some fair flower, all loveliness in
    place,
A bud of beauty breathing joy on willowy stem of
    grace ;
Her voice was low and lovely, as some rare old
    Spanish tune,
And her laugh was full of music as a mocking-bird
    in June ;

Her smiles were pure and pensive, as moonbeams
    on a stream,
While her face possessed that beauty which gilds
    an Inness dream ;
Indeed she was a Venus, such as Titian ne'er
    could paint,
And her life was one sweet sermon, filled with
    precepts for a saint ;
Oh, she seemed a queen from heaven, and if earthly
    angels be,
Montclair should sing hosannahs for the lovely
    Rosalie.

Her father was a merchant doing business in New
    York,
With a high commercial rating for integrity and—
    pork !
And the lovers came a-courting with their vapid
    city airs,
And an eye, perhaps, for spending her father's
    bonds and shares.
But she sent them all a-sighing to " Hoboken " or
    " Soho,"
Till at last there came a wooer who made her bosom
    glow.
He was gay and brown and handsome, with a wild
    and woolly air,
And he came from Corpus Christi on a lively
    bronco mare.
You would take him for a winner from the way he
    " sot his horse,"

You'd " put your money on him " when he " can-
    tered round the course " ;
Yet with all his " Western manners " he was noble,
    brave, and free,
And she liked his honest purring, did the lovely
    Rosalie.

She was tired of simpering fellows and dudes which
    fashion rears,
And she listened now with shudders to tales of
    snakes and steers ;
For he told her 'bout the prairies and ranches far
    away
Where the centipedes are wooing the tarantulas at
    play,
Where the rattlesnakes are basking in the sunshine
    on the sod,
While the drowsy plains are breathing an azure
    dream of God.
Where the birds are always singing in that breezy
    blossomed land,
Near his cactus hacienda on the tawny Rio
    Grande.
Then he hinted of adventures and the wealth that
    he'd amassed,
Till at length the maiden " loved him for the
    dangers he had passed " ;
Oh, his bosom swelled with rapture, deep as the
    tropic sea,
As he wooed this gentle lady, the lovely
    Rosalie.

Though he looked so rough and ready and appeared
    a little wild,
He had great respect for women and was docile as
    a child ;
But he scorned ignoble actions and all motives
    that were mean,
For he 'd breathed the breath of heaven in a land
    where God is seen.
And he hated false pretensions which the crooked
    city broods,
For he learned his truths from Nature in the lonely
    solitudes ;
Yes, his heart beat high but kindly, and affection
    strongly ran
Through the beatific bosom of this "natural noble-
    man."
So he wooed and won that blossom, the flower of all
    Montclair.
And you 'll hear the happy sequel if you ever visit
    there,
For he was a gallant lover, while his bride was fair
    to see,
And New Jersey now is mourning for the lovely
    Rosalie.

A COWBOY TO KIPLING.

On reading his newspaper articles attacking the West.

HUH! Kipling, we ar unto yew—
  We seen yer fairy tale
About our Wild and Woolly West,
  Hence we ar on yer trail !

We liked yer stories uv the hills,
  For they wuz strong an' strange ;
But when yew hit Chicawgo town,
  Yew really missed yer range.

Thar want no Injuns in her streets
  Like yew had hoped tu find,
An' 'cordin' tu the way yer writ,
  Her pace jest knocked yer blind.

We noticed heow yer floundered 'round
  When yew hed lost yer cue—
An' strange tu say, we likewise found
  Yer English wuzzent true !

We know thet we kin " whip the world,"
  An' beat yer yachts hull down,
For all the world acknowledged this
  At New York an' Yorktown !

So stop yer swellin' ! pull yer freight—
   Fer India an' the brush ;
Az Yankees hyar in every State,
   Iz sick uv Kipling slush !

Yes, sah ! we 're tired of Tenderfeet
   Awritin' up our West.
Yew fellers 'lows she can't be beat,
   So give the kid a rest.

We know yer like this country, sah.
   Great Scott ! yer make us laugh !
Yew bawlin' *Gringo from the East*
   Yew *Maverick Indian calf !*

Hit haint no us' ter pitch an' rar,
   Fer Texas hez the sand
Tu rope yer tu her saddle bow
   An' burn yer with thet brand !

———

A SUMMER GIRL.

SHE was queen of the hotel veranda,
   " An heiress," 't was said, " from New York " ;
The dear chappies " could not understand her,"
   But her beauty made every one talk.

Oh, she ruled and she jilted and charmed me,
   And kept my sad heart in a whirl,
And my feelings they really alarmed me,
   For I lived, " don't you know," for that girl.

But the summer went by and we parted,
 And the season swept on to an end ;
To the city I went broken-hearted,
 To dream of my heiress and friend.

EX-PARTE.

Weeks after, when snowflakes were flying,
 I strolled through a Fourteenth street store,
Where I heard my divinity crying,
 "Cawsh, heah ! Hurry up, Twenty-fouah !"

———

BEYOND THE HARBOR BAR.

SINCE thou must sail the seas of life,
 Where storms and billows are,
Steer for that blessed Port of Peace
 Beyond the harbor bar.
Keep to your course ! Sail bravely on
 Toward mansions Over There !
Have Truth and Kindness for your crew,
 And Hope the pilot fair.

Avoid the ragged rocks of Doubt ;
 Doubt is a dangerous reef !
Tack well off shore, stand boldly out
 Past shoals of Unbelief.
Beware that narrow channel, Creeds !
 Keep to the ocean broad,
Where Charity swells deep with deeds
 Wide as the heart of God !

Starboard your helm—reach for the right !
 Keep watch above—below !
Fly loyal colors to the breeze,
 No matter what gales blow.
Sail bravely on—the beacon lights
 Are shining now afar,
Within Love's blessed Port of Peace,
 Beyond the harbor bar.

———

THE TWINKLE OF HER EYES.

BENEATH dark curving lashes,
 Half-hidden from the sight,
Behold those radiant flashes,
 Those gleams of curtained light.
Their lustre gilds life's shadows
 Like gleams from starry skies.
Here 's to my lady's twinkle—
 The twinkle of her eyes.

Sly Cupid owns her glances ;
 He barbs his arrows there,
For love hurls piercing lances
 From orbs of Beauty rare.
Though Youth and Hope may wither,
 Fond Memory still will prize
My lady's laughing twinkle—
 The twinkle of her eyes.

Had I some poet's power
    To sing that witchery well,
What wealth of songs I 'd shower
    To breathe their mystic spell—
What musical romances
    Of fabled loreleis
Would echo of that twinkle—
            The twinkle of her eyes.

TO DIVES.

THEN what of your silver and gold or estate
    When the last trial balance is cast ?
The sums are the same—you may learn it too late—
    But the nickle that laughs on the cold coffin plate
Will be all that you have at the last !

So strive for that wealth that is purer than gold,
    Wealth beyond all the cash of your mart—
Its values are boundless, they cannot be told,
It is prized above rubies but not bought and sold—
    'T is the wealth of a kind noble heart !

AN APRIL SONG—TO ALICE.

THY world is bright, fair Alice,
    Youth's April flowers are thine ;
Thy form is Beauty's palace,
    Thy bosom Pleasure's shrine.

Rare are the rosy showers
　　Which hope around thee flings,
And gay the gilded hours
　　When Love forever sings.

But ah ! proud, pensive Alice,
　　Youth's April cannot last,
And Memory's shrouded chalice
　　Soon claims Life's radiant past ;
And though thy charms may cherish
　　The richer tints of June,
They blossom but to perish,
　　Alas ! alas ! too soon.

There is a sigh of sorrow
　　In every autumn day,
Which whispers that to-morrow
　　Earth's bloom must pass away ;
Aye, youth's warm hopes will wither
　　Beneath Time's chilling beams,
And age has naught to gather
　　But memories of youth's dreams.

So cull life's April pleasures,
　　And kindly act your part ;
For kindness plants rare treasures
　　In gardens of the heart.
Then in thy calm December,
　　'Midst Love's rare twilight rays,
All hearts will still remember
　　To bless thy years with praise.

NEPTUNE'S STEEDS.

HARK to the wild nor'easter !
   That long, long booming roar,
When the Storm King breathes his thunder
   Along the shuddering shore.
The shivering air re-echoes
   The ocean's weird refrain,
For the wild white steeds of Neptune
   Are coming home again.

No hand nor voice can check them,
   These stern steeds of the sea,
They were not born for bondage,
   They are forever free.
With arched crests proudly waving,
   Too strong for human rein,
The wild white steeds of Neptune
   Are coming home again.

With rolling emerald chariots
   They charge the stalwart strand,
They gallop o'er the ledges
   And leap along the land ;
With deep chests breathing thunder
   Across the quivering plain,
The wild white steeds of Neptune
   Are coming home again.

Not with the trill of bugles,
　But roar of muffled drums
And shrouded sea-weed banners,
　That mighty army comes.
The harbor bars are moaning
　A wail of death and pain,
For the wild white steeds of Neptune
　Are coming home again.

Well may the sailor women
　Look out to scan the lee,
And long for absent lovers,
　Their lovers on the sea.
Well may the harbored seamen
　Neglect the sails and seine,
When the wild white steeds of Neptune
　Are coming home again.

How sad their mournful neighing,
　That wailing, haunting sound ;
It is the song of sorrow,
　A dirge for dead men drowned.
Though we must all go seaward,
　Though our watchers wait in vain,
The wild white steeds of Neptune
　Will homeward come again.

CHRISTMAS COVE, Maine, 1892.

ACROSTIC—EASTER BLOSSOMS.

ALICE—MAY—ANNA.

A LICE is a rosebud, a blossom on life's sea,
    Like the fair Aurora a rising queen is she,
In realms of youth and fashion her beauty will amaze;
Command rare royal homage from all who chance
      to gaze,—
Enduring joys, fair Alice, I fain would sing thy
      praise.

May is a calla lily, a bud surpassing fair,
Alluring, coy, elusive, as sunbeams wooing air;
Yes, May 's a lovely lily, a flower beyond compare.

Anna is a violet, that blooms at early morn,
'Neath jewelled dew-drops kisses where lissome love
      is born,
No selfish thought attends her, rare loveliness she
      seems,
Ah, Anna is my ideal, the idol of my dreams.

EVENING ZEPHYRS.

F AR, far away o'er the western horizon
    The sun sinks to rest on a couch of pure gold,
And night spreads her mantle far over the moun-
    tains,
    As the star-spangled banners of heaven unfold.

Alone in my hammock, alone by the water,
   Where soft southern zephyrs steal in from the sea ;
When moonbeams are dimpling the face of the
      ocean,
   Ah, then comes the hour of sweet reverie.

Then the busy old world is well-nigh forgotten,
   The dark clouds of life have all vanished away,
And the beacons of hope shine afar in the future,
   As bright and as clear as the lights o'er the bay.

Then rare pensive music sweeps over my heart-
      strings
   As rare and as pure as the mocking-bird's tune,
When it sings in the twilight alone 'mid the palm
      trees
   Where the pale southern cross woos the shy,
      crescent moon.

Then a proud, pensive face from the Mexican
      border
   Steals again to my side 'neath a magnolia tree ;
And the river, the mesa, the old hacienda,
   Are the same as of old when my sad heart was
      free.

But that 's long ago, and alas ! it 's all over ;
   The past cannot be ; let the future be bright.
So farewell, my lost one, my fair senorita,
   One long last farewell and a kiss of good-night.

ATLANTIC HIGHLANDS, N. J.

THE RANCHMAN'S SONG.

A FAR from the tumult and turmoil of fashion,
   Away, far away, from the throng that intrudes;
I am free from all envy and malice and passion,
   For my spirit expands in the wild solitudes.

I love the broad prairie, the norther's sad sighing,
   The whispering stars, and the owl's lone hoo,
The mocking-bird's song when the twilight is
     dying,
   The cayote's weird call as it echoes "ki-oo."

Wild nature to me is a thing that I cherish;
   I hate the dull discords that cities have shown;
For there out of tune my free spirits all perish;
   Let me dwell near to nature with my ideals alone.

Better live rich at heart on a crust in a garret,
   Than languish in mansions impoverished with
     strife;
There is joy in a dugout, if fancy but share it
   With hope and fond memory to brighten thy life.

There 's a zest amidst hardship which some natures
     treasure,
   A charm on the prairies that care cannot cloy;
So, avaunt! ye dull follies of fashionable pleasure,
   Give me the wild pleasures that ranchmen enjoy.

A MESSAGE.

PRETTY blossom on the prairies, where the
breezes play,
Dost thou know my lovely lady, hast thou seen
her—say ?
She is like thee in her beauty, for her eyes are
violet blue,
And her cheeks are fairest lilies which the roses
love to woo.

Mocking-bird that singeth gayly midst the bowers
of spring,
Dost thou know my bonnie lassie, hast thou heard
her sing ?
She is like thee, always happy, and her voice re-
sembles thine,
Ah ! her laugh 's an airy echo of thy liquid notes
divine.

Lovely sunbeam, kissing beauty, blessings on thy
ray,
Dost thou know *my blushing beauty*, hast thou kissed
her, pray ?
She is like thee, gleam from heaven, pure and
cheerful as thou art,
And she blesses all who know her, with the sun-
shine of her heart.

4

Perfumed zephyr, softly sighing, o'er the tropic sea,
Take this message to my lady, waft it now from
    me.
Woo, oh ! woo her, sigh it ever, breathe my story
    in a line ;
Softly tell her that I love her, gently ask her to be
    mine.

A KING'S DAUGHTER.

A. G. C.

SHE is pretty as a picture,
    She is gentle as a fawn,
She is radiant as the sunbeams
    That kiss the lips of dawn.

She is fairer than the flowers
    That dream of tropic seas,
She is purer than the zephyrs
    That woo the orange trees.

She is winsome as a fairy,
    She has gentle, kindly ways ;
And sweet lips ever ready
    To speak another's praise.

She has higher aims than fashion,
    She is noble, kind and true ;
She believes in " helping others,"
    And the good that she can do.

She is thoughtful of her mother,
  She 's a blessing from above ;
Yes, her life 's a gentle sermon,
  Full of hope and joy and love.

She is cheerful as the sunshine,
  She is kind to everything ;
She is lovely as an angel—
  She 's a " Daughter of the King."

TO MAY IN PARIS.

M. H. C.

SHE 's a lovely fairy fay, is my pensive Cousin
   May,
     She 's divine.
She is gentle, she is wise, yet there 's laughter in
  her eyes,
     Beauty's shrine.

She has lovers by the score, beaux and cavaliers
  galore,
     In her train.
Ah, they woo this lovely prize, with sad looks and
  wistful sighs,
     But in vain.

Lo, I see her now afar, as she wins from her
  guitar,
     Some refrain.

Where the twilight bells of France echo songs of
    rare romance,
              O'er the Seine.

She 's a wreath of fairest flowers culled from
    morning's jewelled bowers,
             In Life's spring.
And though winter 's here to-day I abide in dreams
    of May,
            Whom I sing.

ECHOES.

ON the lonely tawny prairie
    When the night is still and deep,
And the breathing stars are shimmering
    O'er a landscape rich with sleep ;

Where the mournful night-winds sighing
    Wake the drowsy murmuring trees,
And afar some lonely curlew
    Coos her sorrows to the breeze ;

Theh within my haunted chamber,
    Pensive by the embers' glow,
Then, ah then, come shadowy fancies
    From the vaults of long ago.

Where are they, those hopes and visions,
    Dreams of love and joy and truth ?
Flown, alas ! all, all have vanished
    On the fluttering wings of youth.

Where are they, those fond old faces,
  Loved of yore, and oh, so fair?
Where are now those silent voices?
  And the echoes answer—where?

Where all the boughs and blossoms
  Of life's radiant, rosy dawn?
Withered! aye, like rarest roses.
  And the echoes whisper—gone!

THE OLD HOMESTEAD.

TO MR. AND MRS. S. W. SEARS.

ENSHRINED in my heart is an old-fashioned
    homestead,
Alone on the heights, in the woods by the sea.
I love its old rafters and wide, honest chimneys,
Where kindness enkindled warm welcomes for me.
How fair are the faces that often have gathered
Around 'mid the roses that grew by the door;
But the faces will fade, and the roses must vanish,
And the places that knew them will know them no
    more.

How oft in the morn, 'neath the old silver maples,
I have dreamed on that lawn sloping down to the
    bay,
Where I watched the white sails of the out-going
    vessels

Drift on toward the sky, till they vanished away.
Ah, where are the ships of life's early morning,
Youth freighted with hopes and the treasures of
     yore ?
Alas, they have gone, like the barks sailing seaward,
And the hearts that once knew them will know
     them no more.

When the twilight has flown through the flushes of
     evening,
And the moonbeams fall soft on the silvery foam—
What music, and voices, and lovers with laughter
Have dwelt in the fragrance around that old home.
But the music must cease, and the voices grow
     silent,
And the lovers will part when their kisses are o'er,
For the roses must fade, and the faces float sky-
     ward,
And the old homes that knew them will know them
     no more.

DECLINED.

SHE.

" COME back, dear Tom," she wrote to say,
     " To you I 've been unkind ;
So name our earliest bridal day,
     For I have changed my mind."

HE.

" Thank you," writes Tom, " I beg to state
   Your overture 's declined ;
Our wedding 's off—there is no date—
   I too have changed my mind ! "

TO A COQUETTE.

HER wit is like some diamond bright
   Wherein rare powers combine.
'T is brilliant as a flash of light ;
   'T will cut as well as shine.

Her eyes are like her wit, I swear,
   They also play rare parts ;
And Love holds brilliant jewels there
   To gild or pierce our hearts.

She reigns a queen in Fashion's court,
   But wisdom breathes " beware ! "
" A shattered heart is not my forte,"
   And prudence sighs " Take care ! "

Alas ! alas ! She 's too refined,
   Her arts too fair I 've found.
Her wit and charms are all designed
   To dazzle and to wound.

So, lovely lady, we must part.
   'T were vain in me to try
To keep thy hollow, fickle heart—
   I give it up ! Good-bye !

THE OLD TEXAN IN NEW YORK.

TO CAPT. JOHN MILSAP.

HUH ! Sal, this life won't soot me,
　　This russlin' an' these kyars ;
I 'm pantin' fer the praira,
　　The great wide whisperin' stars !
Yew ar a tolerable daughter,
　　Yer Yankee husband 's kind,
But these swift ways uv livin'
　　Don't fit my steddy mind.

This rushin' an' er chargin'
　　Ter me seems powerful strange ;
Thar hain't no grass nor watter ;
　　I 'm lost on this yeer range.
New York 's a human round-up
　　Uv fun an' fuss an' care,
But I 'm er—suffercatin'—
　　I want the broad blue air !

I hate the shows uv cities,
　　They goes ag'in my youth ;
I lov' the tarnal mountains
　　Wot pints tu God an' Truth !
Thar kyant be no decepshun,
　　Whar Nature hews the line ;
I 'm sick uv curvin' fashions,
　　I want things straight in mine.

This roarin' canyon, Broadway,
  Iz drowndin' all my powers ;
Giv' me our lazy rivers
  Wot dreams through seas uv flowers.
Hit hain't no use ter coax me,
  Yer know I 'm powerful sot—
I aim ter quit yer corral,
  Hit 's not my campin' spot.

So, Sal, I 'm fixed ter leave yer ;
  Jes tell 'em all good-by ;
I 'm gwine back tu Texas,
  Ter stay thar till I die.
I 'm lonesum fer the praira,
  The ole home uv my youth,
I 'm needin' uv them mountains,
  Wot pints tu God—an' Truth !

MAN.

"MAN GIVETH UP THE GHOST AND WHERE IS HE?"

MAN lives and dies ! What more know we ?
    With all our pomp and pride.
'Midst wealth or fame or poverty,
  We know this much—" he died."
What lived he for ? To learn, alas,
  That he could nothing know.
To sip the sweets from pleasure's glass,
  Or drain the depths of woe.

We play awhile 'midst childhood's dreams
  Or muse in youth's gay bowers,
Then glide along on time's swift streams
  Through sunshine or through showers.
At length 'midst manhood's billows cast
  We battle trouble's waves
Which sweep us on, we learn at last,
  To quick-forgotten graves.

Fair budding youth and fruitful age
  And beauty's radiant bloom
Are closely twined in life's dim stage,
  And destined for the tomb.
We can not know just what we are,
  Nor dream of what we'll be ;
We know this much—man giveth up
  The ghost, then where is he ?

THAT LITTLE BOY.

HIS merry voice is silent now,
  His hat is hanging there,
And yet I see his wistful eyes
  And sunny, waving hair.

To-night I hear his voice again,
  That laugh of love and joy—
His pouting sighs—those words of pain,
  "Iz I a naughty boy ?"

Once more I see his noble brow
  And tangled, curly head,
Oh, how I long to kiss him now
  Within his trundle-bed.

The sturdy horse he used to pet
  Stands by his silent drum.
His woolly dog is waiting yet—
  Oh why then don't he come?

Alas! he's gone far, far away,
  To heavenly mansion's fair.
He romps no more, he's tired of play—
  He's dreaming—"Over There."

———

A SERENADE.

DEAR lovely lady, dream no more,
  Unclose thy radiant eyes,
The moonlight gilds the lonely shore,
  Night's jewels crown the skies.
Here, here alone beside the sea,
  Beneath yon shimmering star,
I tune my slumbering lyre for thee,
  And touch the light guitar.

Hark! hear the soft vibrations ring
  Upon the listening air,
To thee I play, my love, and sing,
  Oh, do not slumber there ;

The wooing zephyr breathes its sighs,
  Sad sobs the whispering sea,
The lonely echo's wail replies,
  All Nature longs for thee.

So leave thy couch and heavenly dreams,
  Come where the lilies bloom,
Come while the night's rare pensive beams
  Are lost in flowered perfume.
For here alone beside the sea,
  Beneath yon listening star,
I tune my slumbering lyre for thee,
  And touch the light guitar.

TEXAS.

TO JUDGE A. H. WILLIE.

I CRAVE not for her cities
  Nor towns where man hath trod,
But I love her lonely prairies,
  Her great wide skies of God.

I love her lazy rivers
  That wed the Mexique Sea,
And oh, her heaven-born breezes
  Breathe rarest songs to me.

Oh, if I could but sing them,
　Could hymn pure Nature's bars,
Those songs would live forever
　And echo through the stars.

Would echo till the angels
　Attuned the free refrains,
And breathed celestial music—
　The poetry of the plains !

I love the *Mesa* Mountains
　That woo the Texas skies,
'Neath azure veils of beauty,
　They dream of Paradise.

I love her sweeps of distance,
　Her drowsy miraged seas,
Her choirs of singing songsters,
　Her weeping bannered trees.

And when the sunset's laces
　Befringe the couch of night,
I love her royal pictures
　Of far eternal light.

Oh, if I could but paint them,
　Could hint the twilight's art,
What scenes of heavenly splendor
　Would gild each human heart.

Vain, vain such fond ambition,
　Man is but earthy sod,
His efforts are as nothing
　Beside the works of God.

Yes ; you can have the city,
　Its fuss and fun and care,
Give me a life of freedom,
　'Midst castles in the air !

Your operas' stifled music
　Contains no songs for me,—
I want the vibrant breezes,
　The anthems of the sea.

Give me the low of cattle,
　The cayotes lone "ki-oo !"
The sighings of the Norther,
　The owls' "whit-tu-woo !"

I ask not for companions
　Whose presence might intrude ;
My dearest friend is Nature,—
　I love the solitude.

Ah, who would then be richer ?
　My wealth is all divine—
The clouds, the stars, the prairies,
　The world, the world, is mine.

THE YACHTSMAN'S SONG.

TO LEWIS QUENTIN JONES, NEW YORK YACHT
CLUB.

HO, comrades !   Up anchor !
   Set sail and away—
The tide is now rising,
   There is life on the bay.

The first flush of morning
   Illumines the clouds,
And a fair wind from heaven
   Is wooing the shrouds.

The lapping wave ripples
   And kisses the side ;
Our vessel swings seaward
   To stem the flood tide.

The mainsa'l is flapping
   And tugs at the mast,
The traveller is rattling,
   The breeze freshens fast.

Our bowsprit is plunging—
   It longs to be free,
The billows are rolling,
   Hurrah for the sea !

Haul taut the peak halyards,
  Stand fast at the wheel !
The water scuds past us
  And boils at the keel !

Let go on the mainsa'l,
  Look out for the boom—
Ye gods, this is glorious !
  This briny perfume.

She heels to the starboard,
  Hurrah for the spray !
Like a seabird of morning
  She is off and away !

WOULD N'T YOU ?

I MET her at dusk 'midst the clover,
  In the old orchard path by the sea.
She blushed as she turned to walk over,
  Then shyly stood glancing at me.
She was fair as the flowers of morning
  And pure as the first breath of dew,
So, while her rose flushes were dawning
  I—well, it 's no matter to you.

Sly Cupid had well planned the meeting,
  For love lingered nigh on the breeze ;
And the twilight observing my greeting
  Returned a warm kiss to the trees.

"LIKE A SEA-BIRD OF MORNING SHE IS OFF AND AWAY."

As the zephyrs were wooing the ocean,
　And the doves were beginning to woo,
And the world seemed intense with devotion,
　I—well, it 's no matter to you.

The soft evening shadows soon found us,
　While the clover breathed forth its perfume ;
And Night drew her curtain around us
　And left us alone in the gloom.
What I told her you will not discover—
　'T was a story that ever proves new,
For I—well, I was her lover,
　And I kissed her, of course ! Would n't
　　you ?

———

THE PARSON PICKAX GRAY.

IN ole days in Californy, in the yar uv forty-nine,
　When we russled round the diggin's fer golden
　　yeller shine,
When money wuz er plenty an' fellers all wuz flush,
An' times wuz jest a whoopin' an' life wuz full uv
　.rush ;
When "likker flowed like watter," an' monte men
　wuz gay,
'T wuz then I knowed the parson, the " Parson
　Pickax Gray."
This dom-nee " rid the circle " jest " slinging' out
　the word,"
　5

An' when he pozed fer preechin', the grimy sinners
    heard ;
Fer the parson wuzzent fancy in his labors fer the
    Lord,
No, sah ! he 'd thunder at 'em like a howitzer of
    God !
He wuz chuck full uv the spirit, the plain an'
    honest kind,
An' he 'd sway his miner aujence like a forest in a
    wind,
Fer his heart wuz full uv feelin's for his strugglin'
    feller-man,
An' he 'd chip in his last dollar ter help him "dust
    his pan."
But he never thought uv givin' fer the sake of
    winnin' fame,
Like speculatin' sharpers investin' fer a name !
No, sah ! he give hit nateral, ez fair an' square an'
    free,
As breezes from the Rockies that sweep the west-
    ern sea ;
An' he wuz allers happy, fer he did the best he
    could
Ter practise all his preechin' in tryin' ter do good.
Yet he sized up every feller accordin' tu his worth,
He knowed the rich pay gravel from false pre-
    tendin' earth,
An' he 'd give each man full credit in perportion
    to his weight ;
Then he 'd round up every rascal till he 'd pull his
    wicked freight,

Fer he wuzzent 'fraid of nothin'—he wuz bound to
    have his say,
Oh, he give 'em straight religion, did that " Parson
    Pickax Gray."

Though he had no fancy pulpit, or church with
    lofty spire,
He corralled crowds uv sinners, an' giv' 'em all—
    hell fire !
He'd crawl upon some bowlder, or mount an ole
    tree stump,
Shufflin' through his Scriptur' deck until he'd cut
    his trump !
He'd loosen out his buzzum, fer he seldom wore a
    coat,
He'd ante up, then deal his text an' preech with-
    out er note ;
He'd crevice through the Bible, an' mine hits
    wealth untold,
Then shovel out salvation in nuggets uv pure gold.
His truths would roll like thunder around thet
    human sod,
Till at times he seemed transfiggered an' peered tu
    " walk with God."
Oh, he pruned thet human vineyard an' driv' his
    gospel pick
Through the bed-rock of perdition till he made
    the devil sick !
An' the boys yelled hallelujah ! an' ole sinners
    crossed the line—

Huh ! I tell yer, that wuz preechin' in them days
    of forty-nine.
His prayers wuz like a cloud-burst upon Sin's
    mountain height,
They 'd wash them delvin' miners out uv darkness
    inter light,
Till they clutched the Rock of Ages an' hauled
    theirselves ashore,
An' quit Sin's gloomy gulches an' sluiceways ever-
    more.
An' when we sang the finish to "Praise Him Here
    Below,"
A shimmerin' halo drifted 'round that aujence 'bout
    ter go.
Then cum the benediction ; that wuz his greatest
    charm,
A soothin', heavenly rainbow uv peace an' love an'
    balm.
Thet wuz a preecher fer yer, that acted out his
    part ;
He wuzzent much on polish, but panned out in
    his heart.
And when the Great Jehovah shall come at Judg-
    ment Day
He 'll call that good ole feller, " The Parson Pickax
    Gray."

A SAN ANTONIO MEMORY.

IN old San Antonio city,
  Where the soldiers' bugles blow,
Dwelt a lady proud and stately,
  Years and years and years ago.
Dark was she, this Senorita,
  Lovely as some queen of Spain,
And her voice was soft, and sweeter
  Than the songs of summer rain.

There she lived beside a river,
  Where the winding waters flow
On and on and on forever,
  To the Gulf of Mexico.
There in dreams of Spanish splendor,
  Midst a grove of stately trees,
Stood her gray old hacienda,
  Home of birds and flowers and bees.

Ah, that dear, old-fashioned garden
  With its wealth of rare perfume,
Seemed of old a glimpse of Eden,
  Lost in tangled bowers of bloom.
There the night-winds sobbed their stories
  Round some lonely little mounds ;
There the mosses' drooping glories
  Draped a family's burying-grounds.

There of old we often pondered,
   Listening to the waters flow ;
There of old we talked and wandered,
   Years and years and years ago.
Oft when twilight's kiss was stealing
   O'er the skies in golden beams,
And the mission bells were pealing
   Vesper songs of poet's dreams,

We would seek some seat embowered
   'Neath the old magnolia trees,
Where the zephyrs' kisses showered
   Rarest fragrance to the breeze.
There we dreamed beside that river,
   There we heard the bugles trill,
Till the echoes seemed to quiver
   Through the evening calm and still.

Then my lady of the villa
   Soft would strum her light guitar,
To some tune of old Sivella,
   Or some song from Alcazar.
Ah, those old extravaganzas,
   How they soothed my restless heart ;
Ah, those dreamy, sad romanzas
   From my life will ne'er depart.

But to-night I 'm sad and weary,
   Listening to the Northers blow,
For the wind is wild and dreary,
   And I dream of long ago.

Gone is now that hacienda,
  Gone that garden known of yore ;
Hushed, alas, that voice so tender—
  Hushed, and lost forever more.

———

THE CYNIC AND POET.

A CYNIC once said to a poet,
  " Fie, fie, you gay piper of song ;
Your tunes are all lies, and you know it ;
  You know that this life is all wrong ;
You sing about Hope in gay measures,
  While the Future is shrouded in mist,
How can you keep piping of pleasures
  When you know that they do not exist ?
You know that this life means confusion,
  That time is enshrouded with care,
That joy is a fancied delusion
  Which dwells in a castle of air ;
You know that the world 's full of sorrow,
  That Love is a lost dream of youth,
That Hope is a dream of to-morrow,
  So tell us the Present's sad truth ! "

" Ha ! ha," laughed the gay, jolly poet,
  " The truth is I 'm sorry for you ;
You hate the whole world, and you know it,
  'T is a pity alas ! but it 's true.
And yet the old world does n't mind it,
  It thinks far too much of itself ;

So why not take life as you find it,
  And stop growling there on the shelf ?
Of course there is trouble and sorrow,
  Of course there is sadness and gloom,
But Hope is the beacon to-morrow,
  And Love is life's purest perfume ;
So leave your dry husks, my dear fellow,
  Life's pastures are blooming to-day ;
Grow cheerful, be kinder, grow mellow,
  Believe me, you 'll find ' it will pay.' "

ODE TO THE NORTHER.

THRICE welcome to the Norther,
    The Norther roaring free,
Across the rolling prairies
  Straight from the Arctic sea !
Avaunt, ye western breezes
  And southern zephyrs warm !
Here 's to the cold, blue Norther,
  The stern, relentless storm !

I 'm tired of love and laughter,
  To-night I long for war ;
For the bugle blasts are sounding
  From the heights of Labrador.
"Whoo-hoo ! " the winds are wailing
  Their muffled reveilles,
And 'round my chimney fortress
  Roar angry, shoreless seas.

Wild storms and wants and dangers
　　Will thrill a poet's heart,
And free his Viking spirit
　　Far more than feeble art.
So welcome to the storm wind !
　　The Northers I invoke.
Here 's to the strong, gray weather
　　That makes the heart of oak !

———

THE DYING ACTOR'S SOLILOQUY.

L IFE'S farce is nearly ended,
　　Nature recalls her debt,
I, whom the world attended,
　　The world will soon forget.
　　　My part so full of sorrow
　　　Will end e'er dawns the morrow,
　　　And, ah, 't is vain to borrow
　　One sigh from sad regret.

I, who so long did cherish
　　Rich dreams of joy and fame,
Am doomed, alas, to perish
　　Without a home or name.
　　　No loving lips to bless me,
　　　Nor hands to once caress me,
　　　Nor priest to e'en confess me,
　　I go from whence I came.

The night is dark and dreary,
  The fire burns low within,
And, oh, the world seems weary
  Of so much grief and sin.
    The cold sad rain is pouring,
    The winds and waves are roaring
    Like demons wild imploring
Of demons sure to win.

Slow falls the great green curtain,
  Life's tragedy is done,
For Death must win as certain
  As shines to-morrow's sun.
    The sod and sea will cover
    Each maiden, man and lover,
    And I so long a rover,
Sure rest at last have won.

THE MAINE COAST.

TO HARRY FENN.

COME away, gentle reader, to the cool coast of
    Maine,
Where the partridge is whirring his drum.
Where the red squirrel "chees" in the ragged birch
    trees,
And the air is pure wine from the casks of the seas,
Come away, gentle reader, oh, come.

Here the woodlands and mountains are wed to
    the sea,
And the spirit expands with the view ;

THE MAINE COAST.
OTTER CLIFFS, NEAR BAR HARBOR.

Here in cool shady groves the red Indian roves,
And o'er the smooth waters of beautiful coves
He paddles his birch canoe.

Here the seal and the heron haunt the rocks and
    the waves,
And the ocean is lost in the sky ;
Here the wild aster grows and the goldenrod
    glows,
And life is a rapturous dream of repose,
Hushed to sleep with the sea's lullaby.

Here afar in the offing the proud ships appear
Like pale vanishing ghosts on the lee,
Their bowed sails drift on till they fade and are
    gone
To some far distant realm toward the fair land of
    dawn,
Past the long level lines of the sea.

Ah, these islands and forests all hint of the past,
Of old memories and legends of years,
For the haunted night breeze whispers tales to the
    trees
Of phantom-rigged vessels on shimmering seas,
And of smugglers and bold buccaneers.

Here the sun sets at evening o'er mountains of
    light
Far away beyond rivers of gold ;

Here the tall pine tree's crest fringe the gates of the
    West
And life is a dream, a pure halo of rest
'Midst charms that can never be told.

    BAR HARBOR, Maine, 1891.

"MAVERICK BILL."   .

I MET him at the round-ups on the Double
    Mountain Fork,
This Viking of the prairies, who " never seed New
    York."
He wore a big sombrero and waving raven
    hair,
His eyes were winter sunbeams and lightning slum-
    bered there ;
He hailed from Mississippi, from Natchez 'neath
    the hill,
But he 'd lived " yars in Texas "—frontiersman
    Maverick Bill.

Somehow we got acquainted, riding behind those
    steers,
And Bill commenced his talking of days in other
    years ;
He 'd " fit them lively Yankees ! Yes, sah, you 'd fit
    'em too,
If friends an' scads an' niggers wuz bein' took
    from you ! "

He showed me scars of bullets received at Malvern
    Hill,
He'd lost three of his fingers—the soldier, Maver-
    ick Bill.

At last we camped and rested beneath the moun-
    tain's spire,
I staked the broncho ponies, while Bill prepared
    the fire ;
And then the stars came staring upon that lonely
    scene,
The lustrous moon rose slowly, from out the foliage
    green ;
At length we started singing—his voice was rich
    and shrill,—
The list'ning wilderness just rang with tuneful
    Maverick Bill.

He sang the "Swanee River"—he "only knowed
    one part";
He hummed sweet "Annie Laurie," a song that
    touched my heart.
Too soon he ceased, and silence fell softly o'er the
    plain,
Although the mournful night wind still sighed its
    sad refrain.
Wild Nature's son grew gentle, I saw the moon-
    light fill
The manly, rapt'rous bosom of pensive Maverick
    Bill.

Said he to me : "Young feller, I know them stars
    iz eyes
Of angels gone to glory—the glories in the skies;
I 'spect my little mother iz lookin' at me—squar !
She went ter find our Fanny—the fambly's over
    thar !
Sometimes upon these prairies thet I so oft hev
    trod,
I feels so high-falutin'—I kinder walks with God !

"There iz a good Great Spirit—He 's whispered in
    my ear—
An' this iz whar He 's livin', He talks ter-night—
    right hyar !
Some time perhaps I 'll find Him, though thet seems
    kinder strange,
But some day perhaps, young feller, perhaps I 'll
    quit the range !
I 'll go ter Mississippi an' git my boyhood's home,
I 'll live thar by the rivah an' cease ter cuss an'
    roam.

" I 'll hunt my good ole parson an' help him with
    hiz church,
I 'll git them naber's young uns from off their poor-
    house perch,
I 'll find my ole Aunt Sally—she allers called me
    wild—
But still she seemed ter like me—leastways she
    allers smiled

When I stole her fig sweetmeats behind the kitchen
    door,
She never went ag'in me—I 'll pay her back—an'
    more.

" An thar, ah, thar 's another, I loved her, shore an'
    true,
But I wuz rough and reckless, an' wuzzent made
    ter woo,
Ah, she wuz jest an angel, an' I wuz all ter blame,
But ever since my boyhood, I 've loved her jest the
    same ;
An' now ter-night, young feller, I 'd give my life, I
    say,
Ter know thet she iz livin', an' happy far away."

He ceased—the winds came sighing across the
    prairies free,
And wooing slumber kissed the eyes of Maverick
    Bill and me.
The morning light came smiling across the misty
    streams,
And choirs of singing songsters dispelled my airy
    dreams.
I nudged my grim companion—but oh, his looks !
    how strange !
My God ! Bill's songs were over—Dead Bill had
    quit the range !

A BAREFOOTED BOY.

EXHAUSTED to-night by the fire's dim glow
   I unconsciously dream of the past ;
My spirit returns to the lost long ago,
   To youth's visions too lovely to last.
Oh, yes, I recall them—those pleasures I had
   When life was a gay dream of joy.
Ah—I was a *happy-go-lucky* young lad
   When I was a barefooted boy.

I loved the old farm and its gnarled apple-trees,
   The daisies and buttercups there ;
Then life was all music and flowers and bees,
   For I dwelt amidst castles of air.
I remember my sire ! his tough hickory gad !
   Time cannot such memories destroy.
Ah—I was an *active* and *sinewy* lad
   When I was a barefooted boy.

I recall Toney's brook and the cool swimmin' hole,
   The chug ! chug ! of Moran's water-mill ;
No grapes were so sweet as the grapes that we
     stole
   From the vines on Hank Hamilton's hill.
How often I raced with that farmer so mad,
   His temper I seemed to annoy !
Ah—I was a *lively, quick-stepping* young lad
   When I was a barefooted boy.

Ah, what a brave trapper was I long ago,
  How I made the red Indians fly !
Where are those rich maidens I rescued from woe ?
  Old Sleuth, a detective, was I.
And where is the queen that my boyish heart had,
  Who treated my love like a toy ?
Ah—I was a *foolish, romantic* young lad
  When I was a barefooted boy.

I remember the neighbor's stray Sir Thomas cats,
  And my fights with the hired man's son ;
That school exhibition, where I hollered out—Rats!
  And those dogs that I slugged with my gun.
But to-night I am weary, exhausted, and sad,
  The future for me has no joy—
For this yelling infant—of which I'm the dad !
  Will soon be a—barefooted boy !

WHAT IS LIFE?

A H, what is life ? A bubble blown
      Across Time's mystic stream ;
Its secret source, alas ! unknown ;
  Its future—still a dream ?

Ah, what is life ? A selfish hour,
  A thrill of thought and breath,
A bud which blossoms to a flower
  That withers soon in death ?
6

Ah, what is life?   An echo's sound,
 A passing sunbeam's glow,
A search for something never found,
 A pilgrimage of woe?

Ah, what is life?   A shoreless sea
 That 's swept by gales of sorrow,
A tear perhaps to-day for thee,
 Oblivion for to-morrow?

No ! life 's a river broad and deep
 That flows to fairer seas
Through pale mysterious realms of sleep
 To God's eternities.

———

I 'M SAD TO-NIGHT.

RONDEAU.

I 'M sad to-night—alone am I
 Where weary sea-birds soar and fly
Around a dreary, brooding shore
Where grieving billows wail and roar
Beneath a gloomy sky.
 "Farewell," the lonely zephyrs sigh ;
 The autumn winds all breathe "Good-by."
 So while the leaves and torrents pour,
  I 'm sad to-night.

I would that thou, dear girl, wert nigh
To cheer me with thy radiant eye.
But no, alas! thou comest no more,
Too soon, too soon my dream was o'er.
Too well thou know'st the reason why
       I 'm sad to-night.

WHO KNOWS?

A SONG.

THROUGH the meadows she is coming,
   Where the birds and bees are humming
      Songs of June.
From beyond the daisies swinging
Drifts the song my lady 's singing—
      A love tune.

How the dewdrops dance and glisten,
How the landscape seems to listen
      While she sings!
Ah, her voice is pure and airy
As the trillings of a fairy,
      How it rings!

See the sunbeams dance and quiver
With delight on yonder river,
      Calm, serene.
E'en the bobolinks and thrushes
Listen now on bending rushes
      To my queen.

Will she frown if I should meet her?
Will she blush if I should greet her
      With a rose?
Will she banish me forever
If I tell her that I love her?
            Ah, who knows!

A TEXAS "LAMB," OR THE COWBOY IN WALL STREET.

I WUZ riz on a ranch in ole Texas, yer know,
    Whar we growed the wild steers an' all sich,
But the bizness plum played—so I thought I 'd
        jest go
    To sum city an' aim to git rich ;
I had heerd uv New York—an' the stockmen up
        thar,
    Them brokers that range on Wall street.
I wuz posted on bulls, I hed carved up a bar,
    An' allowed az I could n't be beat.

I got shet uv my cattle at ole Abilene,
    An' the kyars to ole Gotham I took.
Jee whiz! Wot a town! The sights thet I seen
    Would fill up a powerful book.
Well, I mozied around an' loafered awhile,
    Fer I soon struck a good campin'-spot ;
But at last I concluded I 'd add to my pile,
    Fer the money is thar—to be got.

WALL STREET.

So I went to a feller wot hed a big name
   Fer keepin' uv thoroughbred stock ;
An' when I had studied the neat little game
   I anteed fer quite a peert block.
Well, the market it riz at the big stock exchange,
   An' I seed I wuz playin' to luck.
Now, wuzzent I proud ? I owned the hull range,
   Fer a fortune I reckon'd I 'd struck.

So I kept on a playin', I staked my last lump,
   All my money an' scads from the steers ;
But all uv a suddint thar cum a big slump,
   An' I lost all my savin's uv years.
Then I ciphered an' figgered an' ciphered around,
   Till I give the hull bizness a d—m !
My scads they wuz gone—I pretty soon found
   Thet I wuz "a Texas sheared lamb."

Yes, thet 's what they called me—a peert kind uv
     name—
   Then I seen I wuz green, an' wuz fooled ;
I hed staked my hull wad on some other chap's
     game,
   Some feller perhaps like Jay Gould ;
So I gethered my ole paper gripsack again
   (Thar wuz nothin' else fer me to do) ;
An' I pulled my sad freight to an outgoin' train,
   An' vamoosed the town P. D. Q.

A DRUMMER'S REVERIE BY THE RIO GRANDE.

TO THE BOYS "ON THE ROAD."

THE wild prairie flowers, with their beauty so
    rare,
  Fill the air with delicious perfume,
And the plains stretch away till they melt into
    air,
  In the land where the cactus plants bloom.
Afar from the crowds and their maddening strife,
  All alone on this flowery lea,
I 'll woo gentle Nature, I 'll leave the old life,
  Where the Rio Grande flows to the sea.
I hear, in the distance, the murmuring bees,
  The fold-bells' sweet tinklings nigh,
The tropical zephyrs steal up through the trees,
  And the splash as the river rolls by.

Reclined on her bosom near Nature's warm heart,
  A drummer is lost from the crowd :
No thought of "poor crops" or the toils of the mart,
  Or the cares of a life on the road.
The castles and visions he sees in the sky
  Remind him of boyhood's fond hours,
When life seemed as pure as the white clouds on
    high,
  And the future was lovely with flowers.

No promising merchants who " order next time "
   Crossed his bow in that ocean of peace ;
No rice, and corn bread, and tough bacon rind,
   And beefsteak all swimming in grease ;

No butter as strong as the Sampson of old
   Made him mad in those Sunday-school days ;
No expenses, and excess, and baggage-men bold
   Made trouble in various ways ;
No visions of loveliness, eyes of sky-blue,
   Disturbed then his fanciful dreams ;
No curly-haired fellow (bad luck to him, too,)
   Got away with his pile with four queens ;
No 'busses to catch for the "Midnight South
     Bound" ;
   No trains that are "seven hours late" ;
No dazzling hotel-clerks with looks so profound ;
   No politics changed with each State ;

No listening to stories one thousand years old,
   In those days in the morning of life ;
No open car windows from which to catch cold ;
   No rivals to beat in the strife.
No kind-hearted spinster with gay little curls,
   Whom we 're happy to meet now and then,
Who talks of home influence, and tells all the girls
   To "Look out for those travelling men " ;
All these, my dear reader, and a thousand things more,
   Come back with sweet freshness to me,
As I lie in the flowers, on the cactus-bloomed shore,
   Where the Rio Grande flows to the sea.

It 's a very nice thing when from home you 're afar,
    Thus to follow your fancy's own bent ;
To recline by some river and strum a guitar
    And drift to the Isles of Content.
And if, in the future, old grim-visaged Care
    Shall sail through your fanciful realm,
Jibe your life's bark about, fly your mainsail in air,
    And put happy Hope at the helm—
Sail off from that vessel of doubt and despair,
    Come along, my dear fellow, with me,
And we 'll talk of old times and our castles in air,
    Where the Rio Grande flows to the sea.

———

BRER BROWN'S COLLECTION.

Look hyar, my Baptis breddren,
    Salvation 's free, I knows,
But *I 'ze de Gospil hydrant,*
    Tru which de watters flows.

An' dat dar las' colleckshun
    We 's takin' at de doah,
Won't keep de streems er-flowin'
    Tru dis yeer reserwoir ;

I 'ze tole yer' foah about hit ;
    I preeched de odder day
" *De labrer in de winyard*
    Am worthy uv his pay."

I kyant 'cept no excuses,
  De thirsty mus' go dry,
De *stingy sinners roun' dis throne*
  Won't nebber claw de sky !

De Lord kyant nebber bless yer
  De ways yer 's gwine on ;
Yer 's gwine ter ketch de debbil
  On this hyar Sunday morn.

You niggers like de possum
  Yer gets a powerful heap ;
But tech him (in de pocket)
  Ye 'z shore ter fall asleep !

Yer long-tailed coats kin kiver
  De monstrous ugly patch,
But dey ain't gwine ter sabe yer
  Up dar at Heaben's latch.

You 'll grin an' try yer coaxin',
  But Petah, he doan keer—
He 'll shet de gates an' tell yer
  " You cannot enter hyar ! "

De stall-fed, stingy sinners
  Wot 's feedin' roun' dis throne,
Kyant git no moah redemption
  Widout I gets de bone.

De bacun cums too cos'ly,
  De chickens roos' too high,
Fer me ter furnish stuffin'
  Fer all de Pilgrims' pie.

Dar no moah Bam of Gilead,
  Unless you 'ze got de cash,
An' 'less yer pays fer preachin'
  De Preecher 's shore tu smash !

Dars no moah free salvation—
  I 'ze dun got fraid ter trus' !
An' 'less yer cums up libral
  Dis Gospil 's gwine ter bus' !

So 'member what I tells yer—
  I 'ze bleeged to hab sum pay ;
I kyant 'cept no excuses !
  So, Breddren—Let us Pray !

"REMEMBER THE ALAMO."

TO THE SAN ANTONIO CLUB.

FAIR Greece and Rome brave heroes knew,
    But Texas has her heroes, too,
      The men of Alamo !
That bold, courageous, noble band
Of rangers in the border land,
Who fighting fell with sword in hand,
      At San Antonio !

Their well-remembered woes and wrongs
Demand no feeble minstrel's songs,
  For history's fame is theirs.
Their names shall live on mortal tongue,
Their deeds of valor long be sung,
Their memories blessed by old and young
  In silent tears and prayers.

Dark Gettysburg and Waterloo
Survivors from their carnage knew,
  Thermopylæ had one !
But on the Lone Star's gory field
The Texans bled, but would not yield ;
Each man died fighting on his shield—
  The Alamo left none !

Crockett, Travis, and Bowie's names
Shall glow with Freedom's holy flames
  And brighten Glory's sheath !
No lettered urn or flowered perfume
Need mark such storied heroes' tomb,
For honors round their names shall bloom
  In an immortal wreath !

A SONNET TO NIGHT.

THE twilight's laces fringe the sea,
 Whilst far beyond yon mountain's crest
 The lingering, lonely sun seeks rest,
And life seems lost in reverie !

No sound from woodland, shore, or lea,
Save from yon airy sea-bird's nest,
Where fledglings greet a mother-guest
Returned from wanderings wild and free.

Dark spectral fingers clasp the land
And daylight smiles her last good-bye,
Whilst, far beyond the reverent strand,
The vanquished hosts of evening fly,
As night's victorious, restful hand
Flings jewelled banners o'er the sky.

———

LADY BELLE—A VILLANELLE.

L OVELY lady, Lady Belle,
Pray incline thine ear to me
Whilst I sing my villanelle.

Mark and listen, listen well,
As my lyre is tuned for thee,
Lovely lady, Lady Belle.

Hear the music rise and swell,
As it echoes clear and free,
Whilst I sing my villanelle.

Dost forget that twilight dell,
Where to-night I long to be,
Lovely lady, Lady Belle?

There in dreams my fancies dwell,
Dwell in dreams beside the sea,
Whilst I sing my villanelle.

Yes, I love thee ! love thee well,—
Pray *incline thy heart* to me,
Lovely lady, Lady Belle,
Whilst I sing my villanelle.

THE ROUND-UP.

WITH the joy of the wind in our hearts and
    our faces,
  We drive the shy cattle across the divide ;
Hurrah for the zest and the swift, reckless races
  That make up the pleasures of such a wild ride !

Through mesquite and cactus and *chapparral*
    bushes,
  Over oceans of blossoms we gallop along ;
On, on ! toward the round-up our stout broncho
    rushes,
  As we drive up the stragglers with shout and
    with song.

We have searched the lone canyon and scoured the
    valley ;
  We are driving the mavericks, the calves, and the
    steers ;
On, on, toward the outfit, where stockmen all rally,
  To claim hoofed possessions by brands and
    marked ears.

Oh, the roaring and surging and pawing of cattle !
  How they bellow and stampede and long to be
    free !
How their lowered heads crash as they lock horns
    in battle !
  How their billowed backs heave like some wild,
    tawny sea !

While cowboys and "nesters" stand guard on
    swift horses,
  The range boss's outfit rides in through the herd
Cutting out and inspecting—grim, trained, active
    forces
  That divide up the cattle without a waste word.

Each man "holds" his own, then the roping and
    branding ;
  Ye gods, this is sport ! see that yearling career ;
The lasso has caught him ! See that bowed bron-
    cho standing
  As firm as a rock, with his head to the steer.

When the day's work is over to "camp" we are
    flying,
  To unsaddle and hobble and joke with the cook;
When the supper is finished, there's a *round-up of
    lying*,
  But the tales that we tell are not told in this
    book.

DISTANT VIEW OF ROUND-UP.

"CHRISTINE."

Her voice is like the mocking-bird's
   Upon the myrtle tree ;
Her laugh is like the rippling rill's
   That woos the flowery lea ;
Her eyes are like fringed evening stars
   That dream of tropic seas ;
Her breath is like the kiss of morn
   That sighs through orange trees.

The clover loves her nimble feet,
   The zephyrs woo her hair ;
The twilight lingers on her cheek
   In lissome beauty there ;
The roses kiss her budding lips,
   Where laughing pearls are seen ;
All Nature loves dear "Little Chris,"
   For she is Nature's queen !

Ah ! she is like some lily fair,
   All loveliness in place ;
A beauteous blossom, breathing joy
   On willowy stem of grace.
Oh ! may the joys of heaven attend
   This airy, fairy queen,
For she 's the sovereign of my heart,
   This little girl—"Christine."

THE OLD LOG FIRE.

YER kin preech uv the pleasures an' joys uv the
    rich,
  'Bout yer oprees an' parties so gay ;
Yer kin dwell amidst fash'nable folks an' all sich,
    But I don't keer to live theterway.
Giv' me my ole ranch in the wild solitudes,
    Fer uv Nachur I never kin tire ;
Then giv' me sum books and a pipe fer all
    moods,
    An' a cheer by the roarin' log fire.

Yer oprees iz dull tu the muzic I heers,
    When the flames iz asingin' tu me,
An' the big chimbley roars hit's old chune in my
    ears,
    Like sum far-away song uv the sea.
Ah, then with sum feller like Edgar A. Poe,
    Or Shakespeare, who kinder gits nigher,
I mozey 'way back tu the dim long ago,
    Ez I dream by the roarin' log fire.

My ole 'magination jest gits me, fer shore,
    When I loafer around with ole Scott ;
Them Waverley novels I 've read o'er and o'er ;
    His pomes I 've never forgot.

Yer kin liv' in yer cities ef yew are inclined,
  But uv fashion I do not desire ;
Giv' me my ole ranch an' er contented mind,
  An' sum books by the roarin' log fire.

OLD FORT PHANTOM HILL.

(An abandoned fort in Jones County, Texas. Supposed to be
haunted.)

TO THE VETERANS OF THE BLUE AND THE GRAY.

ON the breezy Texas border, on the prairies far
    away,
Where the antelope is grazing and the Spanish
    ponies play ;
Where the tawny cattle wander through the golden
    incensed hours,
And the sunlight woos a landscape clothed in royal
    robes of flowers ;
Where the Elm and Clear Fork mingle, as they
    journey to the sea,
And the night-wind sobs sad stories o'er a wild and
    lonely lea ;
Where of old the dusky savage and the shaggy
    bison trod,
And the reverent plains are sleeping 'midst drowsy
    dreams of God ;
Where the twilight loves to linger, e'er night's sable
    robes are cast

7

'Round grim-ruined, spectral chimneys, telling
    stories of the past,
There upon an airy mesa, close beside a whisper-
    ing rill,
There to-day you'll find the ruins of the Old Fort
    Phantom Hill.

Years ago, so runs the legend, 'bout the year of
    Fifty-three,
This old fort was first established by the gallant
    soldier, Lee ;
And to-day the restless spirits of his proud and
    martial band
Haunt those ghostly, gloomy chimneys in the Texas
    border land.
There once every year at midnight, when the
    chilling Northers roar,
And the storm-king breathes its thunder from the
    heights of Labrador,
When the vaulted gloom re-echoes with the owls—
    " whit-tu-woo ! "
And the stealthy cayote answered with his lonely,
    long " ki-oo ! "
Then strange phantoms flit in silence through that
    weeping mesquite vale,
And the reveilles come sounding o'er the old Mc-
    Kenzie Trail,
Then the muffled drums beat muster and the
    bugles sadly trill,
And the vanished soldiers gather 'round the heights
    of Phantom Hill.

Then pale bivouac fires are lighted and those
    gloomy chimneys glow,
While the grizzled veterans muster from the taps
    of long ago,
Lee and *Johnston* and *McKenzie, Grant* and *Jack-*
    son, Custer, too,
Gather there in peaceful silence waiting for their
    last review ;
Blue and gray at length united on the high re-
    doubts of fame,
Soldiers all in one grand army, that will answer in
    God's name.
Yes, they rest on heights of glory in that fair, celes-
    tial world,
" Where the war-drum throbs no longer, and the
    battle-flags are furled."
And to-day the birds are singing where was heard
    the cannons' roar,
For the gentle doves are nesting 'midst those ruins
    of the war.
Yes, the mocking-birds re-echo : " Peace on earth,
    to men good will,"
And the " swords are turned to ploughshares " in
    the land of Phantom Hill.

GOOD-BYE.

GOOD-BYE, Sweetheart—our dream is past,
  The swallows homeward fly ;
The faded leaves are falling fast,
Our summer joys are o'er at last,
  Good-bye, Sweetheart ! Good-bye !

The wailing winds, the meadows sere,
  The lonely sea and sky,
The naked trees and landscape drear,
Suggest departures for the year,
  Good-bye, Sweetheart ! Good-bye !

The grieving waters woo the strand,
  All Nature breathes a sigh ;
Pale Autumn waves her spectral hand
And whispers to the listening land,
  Good-bye ! Good-bye ! Good-bye !

"REVERIES OF A BACHELOR."

(With apologies to Donald G. Mitchell.)

LONG, long ago, a careless lad,
  The scapegoat of a village,
Who made the rustic neighbors mad
By boyish pranks and pillage ;

'T was then, I say, I knew a lass—
   " A girl beneath my level "—
The daughter of—well, let *that* pass—
   I loved her like—the devil !

I met her at the grammar school—
   That dear old rural college
Where hand in hand through sum and rule
   We climbed the heights of knowledge.
Ah, she to me was passing fair,
   Her smiles were *so entrancing !*
She *was* an angel ! I declare—
   I vow I 'm not romancing.

Ah, yes, she was my fairy queen,
   I worshipped and adored her ;
I praised her charms in verse serene—
   I 'm sure I must have bored her.
I loved the ribbons that she wore,
   The books and slate she carried ;
And now and then I gravely swore
   " That we should soon get married !

At this she laughed and shook her head,
   And said to me *so* chilly,
" You naughty, foolish, stupid Ned,
   You boys are *all* so silly."
Her haughty father's name was Dan—
   He " drove a horse and carriage "
(He drove them—for another man)
   When I had thoughts of marriage.

I told her of my lofty aims,
  The acres of my daddy ;
But she was deaf to all my claims—
  She *loved* a youth named—Paddy !
Oh, how I fought that lusty lad—
  (He walloped me like thunder)
Ah, *then* my boyish heart was sad
  With grief and love and wonder.

But *now* these reveries make me laugh,
  And now I laugh at marriage ;
She is a coachman's better half,
  " They keep a horse and carriage."
Ah, yes ; the fates were kind, I vow—
  We both have won our wishes ;
I 'm *wedded*—to the muses—now,
  And she is—*washing dishes !*

ENNUI.

AT a lonely ranch neath a lonely sky
  On the tawny Texas prairie,
Where the owls hoo, and the plovers cry,
  And the cayotes howl, and the Northers sigh,
    To-night I am sad and weary.
The fire dreams on in its chimney-bed,
  While the rain on the roof is sobbing
A requiem sad for a year that 's dead,
For the shadowy faces flown and fled,
For the days misspent, and the words unsaid,
  And the dreams that Time is robbing.

Without, in the wind and rain and gloom,
   The night is steeped in sorrow,
While spectral fancies haunt my room
With ghostly thoughts from Memory's tomb,
   And the cares of a dull To-morrow.
Ah, Life is at best a lonely lane
   O'ergrown with the rue and roses,
Though the flowers must wither, the thorns remain,
For each heart knoweth some secret pain ;
Some fond regret, and some hope in vain,
   In each secret soul reposes.

Hast thou not sighed for some ideal shore
   'Midst groves and forests vernal—
Where pain and trials and griefs were o'er,
Where the world was fair as dreams of yore,
Where hearts were true and life was more,
   And love was a thing Eternal?
Ah, yes ! and to-night 'neath a lonely sky,
   On the tawny Texas prairie,
Where the owls hoo and the Northers sigh,
Where the cayotes wail, and the plovers cry,
   To-night I am sad and weary.

   December 31st.

THE BRAZOS QUEEN.

FAR down in Southern Texas, where the Brazos
      River flows,
Where the cotton plants are blooming and the
      stately live oak grows,
Where shrouds of waving mosses drape spectre
      cypress trees,
And butterflies are floating through the fragrant
      breathing breeze ;
Where the pensive, pure magnolias dream away the
      golden hours,
And the sated cattle wander through royal realms
      of flowers ;
Where the mocking-birds are singing to the blos-
      soms on the lea,
And this river winds forever to wed the Tropic
      Sea ;
There, in a hacienda midst bowers of foliage
      green,
There lives a gentle lady—the lovely *Brazos
      Queen !*

Her voice is low and tuneful as some airy, sad
      guitar,
Her cheeks are like pale roses from twilight realms
      afar,
Her eyes are like pure sunbeams that fringe some
      mountain stream,

And her face suggests the beauty which haunts a
poet's dream ;
Her thoughts are pure and lofty, as mountain peaks
of snow,
Yet her nature's warm and lovely as the prairie
sunset's glow.
Ah, she's an earthly angel—her name you'll never
guess !
And so, my gentle readers, we'll call her—*R. F. S. /*
Now *R* shall stand for "royal," and *F* may "fairy"
mean,
And *S,* of course, is "sovereign," for she's the
Brazos Queen !

Yes, she's the queen of nature, the song of
morning birds ;
The music of the zephyrs re-echoes in her words.
But now her doves are mourning, her zephyrs too
are sad,
For they have been deserted ! alas, it is too bad.
My lady's left her kingdom—her village subjects
frown ;
For she has gone to conquer the proud and stately
town.
Her gallant cavaleros that roam the Brazos side,
All, all have been deserted,—alone they sigh and
ride.
She took their sunshine with her, to gild a grander
scene,
For now midst courts of fashion she reigns a royal
queen.

Take care, ye city gallants, in spite of all your arts,
This lovely village princess will capture all your
    hearts.
Yes ! yes !   You 'll all be sighing around her
    dainty feet ;
Ye bees will woo this flower, this blossom pure and
    sweet.
And all the lonely zephyrs that sigh around her
    home
Will seek and woo and love her, wherever she may
    roam.
And though she may forget them, her loyal stars
    look down
And dream of her forever, this Venus gone to town.
Yes, e'en the dames of Fashion will leave their
    royal sport
And flock to do her homage—the Brazos Queen at
    Court.

Oh, if my hand could gather fame's laurels for her
    now,
I 'd cull a lovely garland and place it on her brow,
If I could *chain the sunbeams*, could *rope the stars*
    of night,
I 'd give them to my Lady, and crown her life with
    light.
If I could sing such carols as to the birds belong,
I 'd gently breathe them to her and fill her soul
    with song.
Then perhaps amid her triumphs, perhaps she 'd
    not forget

Her absent, exiled minstrel, who dreams about her
  yet.
Perhaps the "Poet Ranchman," who 's doomed to
  dwell apart,
Might hope to live in memory—some Eden of her
  heart.
Oh, may she long be happy, this maiden rare,
  serene,
And may God always bless her—our dainty Brazos
  Queen !

THE WALTZ.

THE wooing waltz, the wooing waltz,
 Still of that waltz I 'm dreaming,
For she was mine that lovely night,
 Was mine at least in seeming.

Within that room, that crowded room,
 So crowded, yet so lonely,
We drifted on, we two alone,
 I thought of her, her only.

Her little hand, her jewelled hand,
 Seemed lightly to caress me ;
It thrilled my heart with pride and joy,
 It seemed to say, " I bless thee."

The music rose, the music fell,
 Now slower and now faster,

On, on we danced, in easy tune,
  Close, closer still I clasped her.

I watched her eyes, her wistful eyes ;
  I breathed through perfumed tresses,
Her dimpled cheeks and pouting lips
  Invited warm caresses.

Her pensive flush, her truant blush,
  Betrayed her inward feelings ;
Those drooping eyes, those gentle sighs
  Suggested love's revealings.

We drifted on, outside the room ;
  Ah, how could I resist her,
For in that dimly lighted hall
  I slyly stooped and—kissed her !

The music dreamed, the music breathed
  The story that I told her,
And in that hallway's friendly gloom
  She listened on my shoulder.

THE HERMIT'S SOLILOQUY.

("There is a solitary hermit living in the Panhandle of
Texas who is known to be a foreign nobleman. He dwells
in a dugout, entirely alone, and refuses to have any inter-
course with mankind. It is said that domestic trouble drove
him from a luxurious home in Europe and induced him to
adopt his present mode of life."—St. Louis paper.)

A FAR on the prairies, afar and alone,
   Where Nature dreams, and the Northers
     moan,
Where the cayote prowls the long night through,
And the owl sighs its sad " tu-whoo ";
Where the gloomy buzzard wheels and flies
On the wings of Death 'neath Southern skies ;
Where the lonely stars shine clear and cold
O'er the weary wastes of a world grown old ;
To-night alone by the embers glow
I am lost in the gloom of a long ago—
Lost midst sorrows which none can scan,
Close, close to Nature, yet far from man.

I, who in youth true friends have known,
Am friendless now, afar and alone,
My hopes abandoned, my dreams undone,
Forgotten by all, cared for by none.
Alone am I, alone with that strife
Which gnaws at the heart of a blasted life.

No love, no hope, no faith—all gone !
'T were better, alas, I had ne'er been born.
For what does it matter—this waste of breath,
This struggle for life, this fight with death ?
Ah ! life 's but a shadow, a shadow in air—
We came from darkness, we go to—where ?

'T were better, indeed, to hope for some sphere
Where the soul may rest beyond sorrows here ;
But my sad heart, so long deceived,
Mistrusts the dreams that it once believed.
Yes, I who in youth had faith above
Have lost all faith through a faithless love.
O God ! that thought—her false, fair face
Still haunts my life in this lonely place.
The pensive charm of her wistful eyes
I see in the depths of the azure skies ;
And oft at night midst the moon's pale beams
She haunts my den and fills my dreams.

Her low, sweet voice I have often heard
In the twilight songs of the mocking-bird.
Lo ! the winter comes and the summer goes,
While the tide of seasons ebbs and flows ;
The spring returns with its birds and flowers
In a dreary round of weary hours ;
The months and years roll by—and yet
Alas ! alas ! I cannot forget !
And to-night afar, by the fire alone,
While the Norther sighs and my spirits groan,
Where the lonely owl calls "tu-whoo,"

And the cayote wails the whole night through,
Alone am I, alone with that strife
Which haunts the heart of a blasted life !

———

NEVER DESPAIR.

GIVE up vain regretting, don't sigh for the past,
Let the veil of oblivion be over it cast ;
Fond memories are pleasant, but they never will
pay,
The sight drafts of Time that fall due on to-day ;
Be up and be doing, don't trifle with Time,
If you long for success you must labor and climb.

Success is a blossom that blooms into life
On the mountains of toil amidst bowlders of strife ;
The paths that lead up to that flower so rare
Are rocky and dangerous, and clouded with care.
But beyond the dark canyons that yawn on life's
slope
There are halos of glory and rainbows of hope.

So never despair ! push on with your schemes,
If they are not successful, indulge in new dreams.
The future still beckons, so do not lament,
For the pale vanished past, or the efforts misspent.
Though tossed by life's tempests and billows of
care,
Steer on toward the stars and the lights " Over
There."

TO KATHERINE.

I KNOW a gentle maiden,
　　A *flower* fair is she ;
As graceful as the lilies,
　　That grow by Galilee.
Her cheeks are like the roses,
　　Such eyes were never seen,
Ah, she 's my pretty cousin,
　　The pensive Katherine.

Her thoughts are pure and lofty
　　As dreams of paradise,
And music swoons enraptured
　　In echoes of her sighs.
Her laugh is like the ripple
　　Of music, too, I ween,
Ah, she 's my lovely cousin,
　　The gentle Katherine.

Her life is full of sunshine,
　　Her heart is always kind,
Her nature 's true and noble,
　　Enlightened and refined.
Oh, I 'm a lucky fellow,
　　Related to—a queen !
The queen of budding beauty,
　　The *blossom* Katherine.

THE QUESTION.

FAIR lady, though proud cavaliers
  Are bending round thy throne,
And waiting there with eager ears
  To do thy wishes known ;
And though thy pure patrician face
  Is proud and passing fair,
Methinks, behind the mask, I trace
  A wistful hint of care.

Though wit and beauty gild the scene,
  And every one seems gay,
Though all is life and joy serene,
  Thy thoughts are far away ;
The swooning roses on thy breast
  Betray no calm delight ;
Alas, their drooping buds suggest
  My lady 's sad to-night.

The viols moan—thy men at arms
  Go proudly whirling by ;
Then why, amidst such royal charms,
  Why doth my lady sigh ?
Stern valor gaily strives to gain
  Thy smiles and make thee glad ;
Alas ! each gallant strives in vain—
  Why is my lady sad ?
8

Too well thy minstrel knows his doom—
   A lonely life of care—
But far beyond the clouds of gloom
   One star is shining there !
For though his sun has long been set
   O'er hopes too fond to last,
He lives in halos of regret,
   The starlight of the past.

Though vain, alas ! his thoughts may be,
   Though doomed to dwell apart,
He lives alone with thoughts of thee,
   The mistress of his heart.
No matter where his footsteps rove,
   Where e'er his lot is cast,
He 's loyal to his early love,
   His first love and the last.

To-night, while sleeping on the plain,
   Beneath star-curtained skies,
He heard thy soft, sad voice again,
   And dreamed of starry eyes.
Oh, yes, I dreamed, lost love of mine,
   Once more I felt thy kiss ;
Once more I dwelt in realms divine,
   In fervent arms of bliss.

I dreamed we two at last were one,
   That through this land of breath
The current of our lives should run
   Down to the seas of death.

That far beyond the clouds of life,
　Above God's azure skies,
That I could claim thee there as wife
　In realms of Paradise.

Alas! alas! it cannot be,
　Vain, vain, each fond regret;
The regal charms beam not for me,
　But oh, I can't forget!
Thy royal path winds far from mine,
　And it is better so;
For thee a grander sun must shine
　Than that of long ago.

A richer suitor seeks thy heart,
　Your old knight could not be
Both bard and Crœsus in one part,
　But still he'd die for thee!
Then is thy sadness now a whim,
　Some idle fear forsooth—
Or is it some fond thought of him,
　The lover of thy youth?

———

YOUTH.

IN the Ocean of Time there's a wonderful isle
　Embowered in roses and beautiful trees,
Where fountains of Fancy all troubles beguile
　And the incense of morning perfumes every
　　breeze;

There Pleasure's gay banners illumine Hope's
  bowers,
 And blossoms of Beauty abound everywhere ;
There Love rules a Queen of the glad, golden
  hours,
 And Life is a dream without sorrow or care.

But, alas ! on that island no mortal abides,
 And the currents flow swift by its perilous
  shore ;
No vessels can anchor in Time's swelling tides,
 They must sail and pass on to return never-
  more.
Do you ask me the name of this beautiful
  land,
 That realm of delight and pleasure and truth ?
Look back o'er Life's billows toward Memory's
  strand,
 Behold it afar—'t is the fair Isle of Youth.

AGE.

L OST, lost, youth's dreams of long ago,
 Flown are the hopes we used to know,
 All vanished into air.
Where are the smiles which Beauty wore ?
Where are the buds which Pleasure bore,
And where the friends beloved of yore ?
 The echoes answer—where !

Why, why this fevered pomp and pride,
This gilded show which soon must glide
 To deep oblivion's sea—
This wealth and power and swelling state,
These smiles of love and frowns of hate,
Soon, soon must flow through "time's wide gate"
 To dim eternity.

Yes, yes, we all are born midst tears,
To struggle on a few short years
 With doubt and dull despair.
Who knows the secret of Life's womb?
Canst thou prove aught beyond the tomb?
Ah! man's brief day is lost in gloom,
 His spirit lingers—where?

Life, life, alas, what worth are ye,
To weary mortals such as we,
 Who long for dreamless sleep?
Our years are scarred by pain and grief,
Our "sorrows neither few nor brief,"
'T is death alone can bring relief
 To aged eyes that weep.

THE "G" STRINGS OF THE HEART.

THIS life iz full uv muzic,
 Hits no use tu talk uv art,
When Old Nacher cums a-fiddlin'
 Roun' the "G" strings uv the heart.

But them dim mysterious poets
  Uv the interlectuool kind,
Had better tune their bugles
  Tu the zephyr flutin' wind.

The world ain't got much leisure
  Fer tu study out a song,
Az the people's all tu busy
  Worryin' how tu git along.
If they cums tu poets' problems
  Thet hez neither sense nor rhyme,
I know from sad experiunce
  Thet they skip 'em every time!

Them meloncholy fellers,
  Wot sings uv woe an' care,
Hed better leave their sepulchres
  An' git out in the air!
Fer wot 's the use uv livin'
  In an atmosphere uv gloom,
Where sunshine never enters,
  An' the flowers never bloom?

The sunshine iz the warmest!
  An' hit "pays the best," I know,
Fer the ole world longs fer laughter,
  Az it has tu much uv woe.
So tune yer wailin' fiddles
  To some lively, cheerful part,
An' let the muzic vibrate
  From the " G " strings uv the heart.

HIGHLAND EVENING SONG.

TWILIGHT blushing o'er the hillside
   Breathes rare kisses to the sea,
Whilst fond memory softly murmurs
   Dreams of other days to me.
Mark the seabird homeward flying
   To its nestling, cooing mate,
While the laughing zephyrs whisper :
   "Love, good night—'t is growing late."

Ah, these shadows silent gathering
   Round this wave-kissed Highland shore
Bring to mind old shadowy faces,
   Faces we shall see no more.
Where are they, the buds and blossoms
   Of life's radiant, rosy dawn ?
Withered—ay, like rarest roses,—
   And the billows murmur, "Gone."

Yes, and we shall soon drift seaward
   On oblivion's unknown stream,
For the sum of all existence
   Is the essence of a dream.
Long these lonely waves shall echo
   Round this haunted Highland shore,
But these scenes and lands that know us,
   Shall remember us no more.

HIGHLAND LIGHTS, N. J., July, 1892.

LINES TO A PICTURE.

MISS EMMA G.

FAIR lady, when at thee I gaze,
  My spirit dreams of other days,
    Of days beloved of yore.
I breathe again that rare perfume
Which hovers round youth's radiant bloom
Ere yet life's bark is wrecked in gloom
    On manhood's billowed shore.

That fair patrician face of thine,
Thy high-born looks and head divine,
    Recall old dreams anew ;
When life's gay current swept along
Through realms of love and hope and song
As free as seabirds' flight, and strong
    And pure as morning dew.

The pensive richness of thy face
Suggests a wealth of inward grace
    Which charms me like a spell.
Thy beauty chains me with its beams,
Thy radiant image ever seems
To haunt my life and gild my dreams
    Far more than I can tell.

As one who worships at the throne
Of some fair idol he has known

In old affection's isles,
Where memory's music softly plays
Midst incense of dead vanished days,
So I now breathe this song of praise
    To bless thy pictured wiles.

FOREVERMORE.

WHEN Aurora's rosy kisses
    Wake the blushing sleeping morn,
And the jewelled dewdrops glisten
    On the silken tasselled corn ;
When the mocking-bird is singing
    To the blossoms on the lea,
'T is then I cease from dreaming
    And awake to thoughts of thee !

When the twilight's golden splendor
    Gilds the mountains far away,
And fair evening's sable banners
    Drape the starry couch of day ;
When the wooing night-winds whisper
    To the lonely listening sea,
'T is then, ah, then, my lady,
    That my spirit yearns for thee !

E'en in morning, or in twilight,
    Or midst dreamland's realms divine,
I think of thee, fair lady,
    For my heart is always thine ;

For like some stream that 's flowing
   Toward the ocean's wooing shore,
So flows my life's deep current
   Toward thee—Forevermore.

BAR HARBOR DAYS.

A LONE, far away by a fire to night,
   Far away on the Texas frontier,
My thoughts have flown backward some months
     in their flight,
   To the glad summer days of the year.
To the days when I met thee—thou vision of art—
   To those Bar Harbor days by the sea,
Though distance dissever, and fate bid us part,
   I 'll remember that summer—and thee.

Have you then forgotten those rare mountain
     rides ?
   Those wonderful views from the shore ?
To-night while the Norther booms o'er the Divides,
   I can hear those wild billows once more.
And have you forgotten those long afternoons
   When we strolled on the rocks by the sea ?
Those days and those rambles, those bass-viol
     tunes,
   Are full of old memories to me.

I remember that hop at the jolly West End,
   Those yachts and our birch bark canoe ;

That ball at "The Kebo," where you were my
  friend ;
Where I dreamed away waltzes with you.
Oh, the scent of that flower which swooned in
  your hair !
 Oh, the grace of your beautiful charms
Was the fairest by far, and the loveliest there,
 When I held you that night in my arms.

I remember your arch doubting look of surprise,
 That soft twilight flush on your cheek ;
Methinks I saw volumes of thought in those eyes,
 Where thy heart is accustomed to speak.
I recall your low voice, like the mocking-bird's
  trill,
 When it sings in magnolia bowers,
And your laugh like the song of the soft-rippling rill
 When it whispers its love to the flowers.

I recall the old song that you sang 'neath the trees,
 Its music I 'll never forget ;
It sighs through my soul like a tropical breeze,
 Which is fragrant with love and regret.
I remember all this, yes, more if I choose,
 Ay, more than I 'll ever confess ;
But you have forgotten it all I suppose,
 And I am just dreaming—I guess.

Yes, dreaming alone by the fire to-night,
 Where the cayotes are calling—" ki-oo ! "

While the sad zeyphrs sigh—" Ah, she never will
    write,"
To a " wild Texas fellow "—like you.
Ah, well ! never mind, perhaps it 's all for the best,
  My fair queen of fashion and men,
For the summer is past—shall I tell you the rest?
  Well—I 've *married in Texas since then !*

MY BARK IS ON THE SEA.

A LYRIC.

M Y bark is on the sea, love,
    My boat chafes at the pier ;
'T is longing there for thee, love,
Pray do not linger here.
Come, let 's away and sail to-day
With breezes blowing free,
With breezes blowing free, love,
Come, let 's away and sail to-day
With breezes blowing free.

I know rare, lonely isles, love,
Where waves the stately palm,
Where softest sunlight smiles, love,
O'er spicy groves of balm.
Let 's woo the breeze for tropic seas,
With Pleasure at the prow,
With Pleasure at the prow, love,
Let 's woo the breeze for tropic seas,
With Pleasure at the prow.

The whispering ripples speak, love,
Rare songs unto my heart ;
The blushes on thy cheek, love,
Fond hopes to me impart.
So let 's away and cruise to-day,
With Cupid at the helm,
With Cupid at the helm, love,
So let 's away and cruise to-day,
With Cupid at the helm.

A SONNET TO THE SEA.

ROLL on, thou proud majestic everlasting Sea !
    Too well thou know'st there is no peace or
      rest ;
For in thy cold, relentless heaving breast
There throbs the great deep heart of all Eternity.
As thou hast been so shalt thou ever be ;
    What dost thou seek—what is thy vain request ?
For thou art grasping still and moaning mournfully,
Why wailest thou ? What is thy mystery ?
    Though feeble man may gaze on thee to-day,
And proudly stem thy breathing, pulseful tide,
To-morrow he has gone ! yet on thy boundless
      billows glide,
    Forgetful of all time, oblivious to all sway,
Save His who rules the world ! whose chariots ride
    Upon the storms ! His whom the winds and
      waves alike obey.

SPRING LAKE BEACH, N. J., July, 1891.

PERSEVERE.

BRACE up, my dear fellow, push on, never fear,
   The victory is thine if you still persevere ;
This life is for progress, don't sigh about luck,
The battles are won by the soldiers with pluck !

No matter how lowly or humble your birth,
Ambition's a merit that 's wedded to worth.
   The world is before you ; push onward and win ;
   If you climb to Fame's portal, just boldly march
      in.

There 's no harm in trying : do the best that you
      can—
Give up useless sighing and fight like a man.
   Aim high and strike hard, leave nothing to chance,
   Don't skulk in the rear, just ride in advance.

Have hope for your beacon forever on high ;
Press forward, keep trying, and never say die !
   So onward, old fellow, brace up, never fear,
   The victory is thine if you still persevere !

TO THE MEMORY OF GEN. SAM HOUSTON.

THY memory is blessed in this proud Southern
    land,
Thy praises are sung by mankind ;
Fair Texas herself is thy monument grand,
Her freedom was won by thy heroic band,
    Her destinies shaped by thy mind.

Thy life and its trials still live in each heart,
    (Youth's romance, alas, was so brief)
Thy story of sorrow surpasses all art,
But thy manhood soon silenced the slanderer's dart,
    Thou hero acquainted with grief.

Then plant the fair flowers around his lone tomb,
    For this hero who suffered and bled ;
O'er his bier let affection breathe forth its perfume,
Let the laurels and lilies eternally bloom
    O'er the dust of the patriot dead.

Sleep on, gallant chieftain; though thou art no more,
    A proud city clings to thy name ;
The future shall echo thy valor of yore,
For History has blazoned thy deeds o'er and o'er,
    On the walls of the Temple of Fame.

Yes ! his name is immortal, but no statue is reared
    By this land that he struggled to save ;

Free Texas should honor his mem'ry revered,
And worship in marble her saviour endeared—
Sam Houston, the noble and brave !

———

TO–DAY.

LET 'S woo the flying hours—to-day,
  While Hope to Pleasure sings,
For who, alas, to-night can say
  "What dim to-morrow brings ? "

The future 's but an empty dream,
  The past returneth never ;
So woo the present's gilded beam,
  And banish woe forever.

Life's fitful shades are fading fast,
  Time's stream soon flows away ;
And youth's swift sun must set at last,
  So let it shine—to-day.

If truth and kindness fill youth's hours,
  Old age will ever be
A garland of affection's flowers,
  Which love shall cull for thee.

Then in the afterglow of years,
  When memory soothes all strife,
Remembrance then can weep no tears,
  For peace shall crown thy life.

Improve the flying hours, to-day,
  For time has winnowing wings ;
And who, alas, to-night can say
  "What dim to-morrow brings?"

———

LINES TO A LADY.

NAY, lovely lady, you are wrong,
  I am not "always gay,"
Nor is my "life a happy song,"
  As I have heard you say.
Ah, no ! I, too, have weary hours,
  But hearts like mine conceal
The thorns which hedge life's scentless flowers
That withered in youth's garden bowers ;
  I do not weep ; I feel !

Though you may think my heart is light,
  Alas, it is not so ;
But still 't is best to make things bright
  In darkest hours of woe.
I know the world is full of grief,
  That life o'erflows with wrong ;
But dull despair won't bring relief,
So I believe 't were best, in brief,
  "To suffer and be strong."
  9

WAITING.

A LAS, for the whim of a proud beauty's ways,
  It is really too sad to believe it ;
I adore her, I love her, I breathe her my praise,
  But her majesty will not receive it.

Ah, once she was gentle and lovely and kind,
  And did not object to my passion ;
But alas for the peace of my heart and my mind—
  I am scorned by this lady of fashion.

I have sued and entreated and suffered in vain,
  But her proud haughty heart is unshaken ;
She is deaf to my woe, she exults in my pain,
  I am exiled, forlorn, and forsaken !

She refuses my love, she " will not be my friend,"
  She refuses me, too, "as a brother " :
Alas, is it over? Is my dream at an end—
  Must I leave her and look for another ?

No ! no ! that is vain, for my heart is still true,
  She, only, controls my affection ;
If she spurns me at last, I shall nevermore woo
  Till—I meet with some other selection.

Ah, yes, I must wait till the wane of the moon,
  Then perhaps she will pity my sorrow ;
Perhaps she 'll relent when she thinks of last June,
  So I 'll wait till—*day after to-morrow !*

MISUNDERSTOOD.

A SONNET.

BURN on, proud soul! no matter the cost—
  Thy destiny to fulfill;
The sun must glow though its gleams be lost,
  It shines and it always will;
So let thy spirit gleam and glow
  O'er the twilight hills of care.
Remember at last though the clouds gloom low,
Though the night seems dark and the tempests
    blow,
  There 's a rosy dawn somewhere!
Thy fate is the fate of a lofty mind—
  How little is known of the good—
To thy worth the world is cold and blind,
Thy wealth is too pure—yes, too refined—
  Thou art Misunderstood.

TEXAS TYPES—THE SHERIFF.

HE 's a quiet, easy fellow, with his pants tucked
  in his boots,
And he wears a big revolver which he seldom ever
  shoots;
He has served his time as ranger on the reckless
  Rio Grande,

And he has the reputation for great marksmanship
    and sand ;
He has strung up several horse thieves in the rust-
    ler days gone by,
And although he seems so pleasant there 's a devil
    in his eye.

When he goes to take a prisoner, he calls him by
    his name,
In that confidential manner which suggests the
    bunco game ;
If the culprit is not willing, takes exception to the
    plan,
Our Sheriff gets the drop, sir, and he likewise gets
    his man ;
Oh, it 's "powerful persuadin'," is a pistol 'neath
    your nose,
"Hands up, you 've got to go, Sam," and Sam he
    ups and goes.

In the fall at "County 'lections" when the candi-
    dates appear,
The Sheriff 's awful friendly, for he loves to
    "'lectioneer";
Then he takes the honest granger and ye stockman
    by the hand,
And he *augers* them for votes, sir, in a manner
    smooth and bland ;
He is generous, brave, and courtly, but a dangerous
    man to sass,

For his manner is suggestive of that sign—"*Keep off the grass!*"

He may run a livery stable, or perchance he keeps hotel ;
He may own a bunch of cattle, or may have some lots to sell ;
He is full of *go* and travel, for he 's paid so much per mile,
And his little bills for "extras," make County Judges smile.
"Hyars lookin' at yer," Sheriff ; come, boys, lets drink her down,
To the most important man, sir ! of every Texas town.

———

TEXAS TYPES—THE CATTLE QUEEN.

IN the lovely land of Texas,
　　Where the "rustlers" seldom vex us,
And the "Legislature checks us
　　With its land laws if you please "—
There, within a hacienda,
Dwells a lady dark and slender,
Who is radiant, rare, and tender—
　　The dashing little widow—Mistress Breeze.

She is pretty as a fairy,
She is gay, and glad, and airy,
Is that queen of the "perairie,"
　　She 's the dearest of our joys,

You 'll surrender when you meet her,
When you see this fair chiquita ;
Yes, you 'll love this señorita,
    It 's the fate of all the boys.

She is graceful as a lily,
But she knocks the stockmen silly
When she rides her lively filly
    Round the ranges after steers.
She can rope a maverick yearling
With her light riatta twirling ;
Oh, I oft have seen it curling
    'Round some bawling brindle's ears.

She owns thirty thousand cattle,
And a bank up in Seattle ;
Oh, she makes the dollars rattle
    When she goes to San Antone—
Oh, I tell you she 's a winner,
Who can cook and grace a dinner
For a famished bachelor sinner,
    That will make his spirit groan.

Yes, she " raises the old Harry "
With the boys—and *likewise Larry,*—
But, alas, she will not marry,
    She 's so "*powerful hard to please,*"
Yet mankind is still her debtor,
For she makes her wild world better,
And I thank God that I met her,—
    This lovely little widow—Mistress Breeze.

TO AN "UNKNOWN FRIEND "—" A. M."

ON RECEIVING HER VERSES AND FLOWERS.

FAIR lady, though we "never met,"
　　Though fate our lives dissever,
Thy kindness I will ne'er forget,
For like some star in Eden set,
　　My heart is thine forever !

Yes, when such kindly acts as thine
　　Illume care's weary hours,
The poet feels that life 's divine,
And fancy's royal rainbows shine,
　　Through all his future showers.

Though like some waif upon time's stream
　　My lonely bark is driven,
Remembrance of thy song will gleam,
And haunt life's drear delusive dream,
　　Like angel notes from heaven.

Thy fragrant flowers are fair to see,
　　Their perfume rare discloses
The gentle thought which prompted thee
To send those lovely blooms to me,
　　Those lilies and the roses.

And though this song but faintly rings
　　With echoes of my feeling,

Remember, lady, he who sings,
Alas ! was born with feeble wings,—
His thoughts are past revealing !

THE RANCHMAN'S RIDE.

HURRAH for a ride on the prairies free,
On a fiery untamed steed,
Where the curlews fly and the cayotes cry,
And the fragrant breeze goes whispering by ;
Hurrah ! and away with speed.

With left hand light on the bridle-rein,
And saddle-girths cinched behind,
With lariat tied at the pommel's side,
And lusty bronchos true and tried,
We 'll race with the whistling wind.

We are off and away, like a flash of light
As swift as the shooting star,
As an arrow flies towards its distant prize,
On ! on we whirl toward the shimmering skies ;
Hurrah ! hurrah ! hurrah !

As free as a bird o'er billowy sea
We skim the flowered Divide,
Like seamews strong we fly along,
While the earth resounds with galloping song
As we plunge through the fragrant tide.

"HURRAH FOR A RIDE ON THE PRAIRIES FREE."

Avaunt with your rides in crowded towns !
  Give me the prairies free,
Where the curlews fly and the cayotes cry,
And the heart expands 'neath the azure sky ;
  Ah ! that 's the ride for me.

THE LADIES—A TOAST.

TO " DI VERNON."

GOD bless the ladies—everywhere—
  And all their lovely graces ;
This world would be a world of care
  Without their winsome faces.
Come ! fill the cup with purest wine,
  Let every lip now press them ;
Here 's to the ladies ! fair, divine—
  Again I say, God bless them !

They brighten all our weary hours ;
  To them the power is given
To make life's pathway bloom with flowers,
  And gild this earth with heaven.
Nay ! chivalry—it is not dead,
  Though knightly Bayard 's perished,
For manhood's shield is always spread
  Toward lovely woman cherished.

Though silent now the troubadours,
  And hushed the minstrels' singing,
All hearts still throb—the poet soars

When Beauty's songs are ringing.
So fill the cups again, my boys,
　　And clink the brimming glasses—
Here 's to the noblest of our joys !
　　Our ladies and our lasses !

———

THE NEW YORK GIRL.

I HAVE known dark señoritas,
　　And proud creole maidens rare ;
I have seen Parisian ladies,
　　And some British beauties fair ;
But of all the royal women
　　That are leaders in life's whirl,
I swear there 's none to equal
　　The dashing Gotham girl.

She is charming, *chic*, and rapid,
　　Full of graces that beguile,
And of all our Yankee maidens,
　　She 's the one that leads in style.
Oh, her dresses are bewitching,
　　And her costume always suits,
For her raiment is " the latest,"
　　From her bonnet to her boots.

Ah, she loves a mild flirtation,
　　For she 's practised all the parts ;
She has read the latest novels,
　　And is up in all the arts.

She 's a cynic and sarcastic,
　　Yet she seldom speaks her mind,
But withal she 's still a woman
　　Truly noble, good, and kind.

So salute her now, " deah chappie,"
　　And remember what I say,
That the New York girl 's a winner
　　From Fifth Avenue to Cathay.
Oh, I doff my old sombrero
　　To this Queen of Beauty's pearls,
And to-night I say, God bless 'em !
　　The dashing Gotham girls !

THE BOSTON GIRL.

SHE usually wears glasses—
　　Has a cool and thoughtful air—
Oh, she "dotes on Browning classes,"
　　And she talks about Voltaire.

She is always craving knowledge,
　　For she dwells in learning's mart ;
Ah, she longs to found a college,
　　Or to start a school of art.

She does not care for fashion,
　　Or the cool New England youth ;
For "science is her passion,"
　　And she only pines for—Truth !

She 's a realist—calm, discerning,
  Scorning everything ideal ;
And her spirit 's always yearning
  For the " realness of the real " !

She has aims and plans by dozens,
  For her nature is intense ;
And she apes her English cousins
  In broad *a's*—and common-sense.

No ! she never is " romantic,"
  And she thinks " most men are fools" ;
For she nearly drives them frantic
  With her knowledge born of schools.

She 's a critic and a teacher,
  And she plays a useful part ;
But, alas ! this cultured creature
  Lets her brains usurp her heart !

THE WESTERN GIRL.

I HEARD the deep bass-viol's cry
  Float through the fragrant night ;
I saw fair angels drifting by
  In youth's purpureal light.

My lips were near her dreamy hair,
  Close to a nestling rose,
That breathed soft incense to the air,
  Blessing such sweet repose.

Her little hand lay warm in mine,
  I watched her starry eyes,
Pure, soft, and rare, deep and divine
  As realms of paradise.

We floated on in dreamy dance,
  Kissed by the wooing breeze ;
My cares asleep in fancy's trance
  Near Heaven's Hesperides.

Oh, could I thus forever tread
  O'er trouble's stormy sea ;
My angel spoke—my ideal fled—
  " *I 'm blowed, let 's quit,*" said she.

―――

THE SOUTHERN GIRL.

HER face is like a tropic sea,
  Soft is her olive cheek,
Her eyes withhold some happy dream,
  She seldom cares to speak.

Ah ! sometimes silence will express
  Far more than prattling words,
And yet her voice is low and sweet
  As song of mocking-birds.

Her pensive smile is like the kiss
  Of moonlight on the hills ;
Her wooing laugh is pure and clear
  As tinkling mountain rills.

She plays the languorous, soft guitar
　　Beneath the orange-trees ;
She knows the songs that zephyrs sing
　　To tropic twilight seas.

She 's gentle, lovely, rare, and pure,
　　The poet's living dream ;
A flower that haunts my memory,
　　A lily on life's stream.

THE CALIFORNIA GIRL.

THERE 's a wild rose breath of beauty
　　　'Bout the California girl,
That intoxicates the senses,
　　And makes the spirits whirl.

She is breezy as the zephyr
　　On the fair Pacific seas,
Yet as balmy as the fragrance
　　Of her blooming almond-trees.

Her laugh is like the music
　　Of those crystal mountain streams,
That ripple through the valleys
　　Of her buoyant land of dreams.

She is gen'rous and impulsive,
　　Has a keen and cultured mind ;
She is bright, and pure, and glowing,
　　With a heart of gold refined,

Her voice is like the echo
  Of some dear old Spanish tune,
While her presence is a garden
  Of the fairest flowers of June.

She 's a royal child of nature
  Cradled by the sunset seas ;
She 's the Queen of the Sierras,
  Wooed by every incensed breeze.

You 'll surrender when you meet her
  (Ah, she gave my heart a twirl),
She 's our twilight señorita,
  Is the California Girl.

THE LADIES OF DIXIE.

IF the ladies of Dixie had marched to the field,
  The war would have never been fought !
Every man had surrendered to such graces re-
      vealed
  And the *Yankees would all have been caught !*

The lilies that bud in the cold, stately North
  Are royal and graceful to see—
But the gentle magnolias that bloom in the South
  Are the flowers of fragrance for me.

Their pure, pensive perfume surpasses all art—
　I care not what others may say,
This Yankee surrenders and yields up his heart
　To the lovely magnolias for aye !

His cannons are silent—all warfare is past—
　The eagle is tamed by the dove ;
My lady of Dixie has conquered at last
　With the wonderful arrows of love.

Our people are one—and the pine woos the palm—
　The palmetto oft dreams of the pine ;
The West for the East has a pure, glowing charm,
　And our union of States is divine.

So let us be kinder—our future is bright.
　Let the war drums forevermore cease.
With shoulder to shoulder, let 's work for the right,
　Controlled by the angels of peace.

THE OLD MACKENZIE TRAIL.

STRETCHING onward toward the sunset,
　　Over prairie, hill, and vale,
Far beyond the Double Mountains
　　Winds the old Mackenzie Trail.

Ah, what thoughts and border mem'ries
　Does that dreaming trail suggest ;
Thoughts of travellers gone forever
　To the twilight realms of rest.

Where are now the scouts and soldiers,
   And those wagon-trains of care,
Those grim men and haggard women?
   And the echoes whisper—where?

Ah, what tales of joys and sorrows
   Could that silent trail relate;
Tales of loss, and wrecked ambitions,
   Tales of hope, and love, and hate;

Tales of hunger, thirst, and anguish,
   Tales of skulking Indian braves,
Tales of fear, and death, and danger,
   Tales of lonely prairie graves.

Where are now that trail's processions
   Winding westward sure and slow?
Lost!—ah, yes, destroyed by progress,
   Gone to realms of long ago.

Nevermore shall bold Mackenzie,
   With his brave and dauntless band,
Guide the restless, roving settlers
   Through the Texas border land.

Yes, that soldier's work is over,
   And the dim trail rests at last;
But his name and trail still lead us
   Through the borders of the Past.

10

LINES TO AN ARTIST IN NEW YORK.

M. T. D.

THERE 's a snug little nook in the city's great
    heart,
  Far above the dull rumble of care ;
'T is the home of a painter—the birthplace of art,
A studio dainty, o'erlooking trade's mart,
  A beautiful castle in air.

There the sun loves to come, and he lingers all day ;
  There the wind sighs its musical bars ;
There the twilight's last kiss gilds the sky far away,
And the zephyrs go wooing the moonbeams at play,
  Where the grim chimneys dream of the stars.

There are curious things in that snug little room,
  Full of pictures and paintings galore ;
There are keepsakes and trophies, and flowers in
    bloom,
Old sea-chests and fish-nets, and jars of perfume,
  And deer-heads hung over the door.

There are pious prayer-rugs and friendly old books,
  Rare orchids in bloom on old plates ;
There are strange little mirrors inviting sly looks,
Low divans and lounges and chairs in queer nooks,
  Suggestive of fond *tête-à-têtes*.

But of all the rare things in that dear little place,
  Of all that fair plunder and pelf,
The fairest of all is a patrician face,
A picture of beauty—an ideal of grace,
  A *study*—the artist herself !

A SONG.

WE are tired of new-fangled verses,
  Oh, sing us some old-fashioned song,
Full of music, and fire, and pathos,
  From a heart that is generous and strong.

Yes, give us a song full of feeling,
  Such rhymes as the Northers rehearse,
Some sonnet of Nature's revealing ;
  We are tired of " magazine verse."

Oh, sing of the rain on the shingles,
  Or the caroling notes of the birds,
And let the deep chords of the ocean
  Resound through the musical words.

Then breathe us the song of the zephyrs,
  As they sigh through the musical pines,
And let the far cry of the sea-birds
  Re-echo again in thy lines.

Oh, sing the pure songs of life's river
  As it flows from the fountains of youth,
Such music is welcome forever,
  For it whispers of Love and of Truth.

Then sing us a song for the people,
　A tune that's unfettered by art,
A song that will make the world better,
　And live in the depths of the heart.

Yes, sing us a song full of feeling,
　Such songs as the Northers rehearse,
Some sonnet of Nature's revealing ;
　We are tired of new-fangled verse.

A MEMORY OF WASHINGTON SQUARE, N. Y.

WHEN I was a bachelor—long, long ago,
　And lived on old Washington Square,
Ah, then I was happy, no care did I know,
　For I dwelt in a *castle of air !*
How well I remember that snug little room,
　With its books and its old easy chairs ;
It was fitted with hangings from Fancy's gay loom,
And Hope was the beacon that lightened its gloom,
　And youth never thought of steep stairs.

There, there all alone, in a tattered old gown,
　With my pipe by the cheerful grate-fire,
I could muse far above the dull roar of the town,
And watch the soft ashes sift silently down,
　As my fancies rose higher and higher ;
There, lost in fond dreams by the embers' warm glow,
　While the smoke curled in clouds through the air,
How happy was I in that lost long ago,
　When I lived on old Washington Square.

I had things in that room with its queer little
   nooks,
  That were full of old memories to me.
There were trophies, and pictures, and friendly old
   books,
Old sabres, and pistols, and rusty old hooks,
  And shells from the Tropical Sea.
But of all the cheap treasures which bachelors
   love,
  There was one which I cherished with care,
'T was a souvenir dainty—a *mousquetaire* glove,
  That hung on the looking-glass there.

And to-night, far away from old Gotham's gay
   sights,
  As I hear the wild blue Northers blow,
I wonder who lives in that room up four flights,
I wonder who smokes by that fire these nights,
  At my castle in days long ago.
Does some jolly bachelor live in that den,
  Does he cherish a soft *mousquetaire?*
Ah, well, let it pass—I am wiser since then,
  Since I lived on old Washington Square.

YE BACHELORS, BEWARE!

SHE is pensive and pouting and pretty,
  She is dainty and dimpled and fair,
She is winsome and wilful and witty—
  But, ah, my dear fellow, beware!

The sunbeam *may dream* of one river,
  Yet it glows on a hundred fond streams ;
It is lovely, but fickle forever,
  Like this maiden who dwells in my dreams.

She is graceful and gay and ascetic,
  She is pure as a vision of air ;
She is cultured and so sympathetic—
  But, ah, my dear chappie, take care !

The roses that bloom in life's morning
  May glisten with jewels of dew,
But they speak to their wooers a warning :
  Remember love's thorns when you woo !

For this dear little lovable maiden
  Is practised in dangerous arts,
And her arrows of Cupid are laden
  With trophies of lost, bleeding hearts.

And though she seems earnest and artless,
  As an angel from heaven, I swear
This maiden, my mistress, is heartless,
  So I bid you, my rivals, beware !

For behold me, a sad, luckless sinner,
  She has robbed my gay life of its ease ;
But I swear by the stars I will win her,
  So, give me a chance, if you please !

For though she seems earnest and artless,
  As some lovely Madonna divine,

Remember, old fellow, she 's heartless.
  (Her heart has surrendered to mine.)

My coquette has tired of folly,
  The ranchman has corralled his dove ;
Soon, soon, we 'll be happy and jolly,
  Bound fast by the lassoes of love !

A BAR HARBOR IDYL.

FAREWELL, gentle lady, the season is o'er,
  The summer's gay flowers are dying,
Like the hopes in my bosom which blossomed of
    yore ;
They wither and perish to blossom no more,
  And regret o'er the landscape is sighing.

You remember that night—ah, that rare night in
    June,
  On the cliffs near the whispering ocean,
Where the light ripples laughed 'neath a silvery
    moon,
And the soft fluted zephyrs sighed love's rarest
    tune,
  How I pledged you my faith and devotion.

You are lovely I grant, you have long ruled my
    heart,
  I have loved you with summer's warm passion,
But alas, my affection is doomed to depart ;

For truth has discovered the depths of your art,
  The arts of a coquette of fashion.

Ah, the harvest is past—'t was a harvest of woe,
  Too long at thy shrine have I tarried,
Pray give back my heart—it was not mine, you
    know,
For this telegram says: " Come and meet me, dear
    Joe,"
  For you see—well, you see—I am married

———

ACROSTIC.

(Birthday lines to the baby boy of Henry A. Chittenden, Jr.,
of the New York *Herald*.)

GOD grant thee much success, my boy,
    And may thy life bestow
New honors on an honored name,
  On that proud name—Gano !

Consider well thy ways in youth,
  Have lofty aims, my boy ;
Invest in kindness, love, and truth—
  These things will bring thee joy.
True worth is more than worldly gain,
  Engage to bless mankind,
New riches then shalt thou obtain—
  Delights the noble find.
E'en then at last, when life is o'er,
  New joys shall bless thee evermore.

THE SHREWSBURY RIVER.

TO MR. AND MRS. LYMAN D. GILBERT.

ONWARD rolls the Shrewsbury river,
  Sweeping proudly to the sea,
Dreaming oft, yet slumbering never,
  Clothed in mists and mystery.

Speak and tell thy tales, O river !
  Tell thy story now, I pray,
Whisper me some olden legend
  From thy realms of yesterday.

Oft when moonbeams fair are flying
  O'er the ivory silver seas,
And the zephyrs sad are sighing
  Through the drowsy whispering trees,

I have heard thy ripples murmur
  Ghostly songs in rhythmic flow—
Of old faces drifted seaward
  In the far-off long ago.

Thou hast heard Atlantic dirges
  And the lonely sea-bird's cries,
Long before the birth of Moses,
  E'er brave Hudson blessed thy skies.

E'er he watched the golden twilight
  Plant her banners starry furled,

Far beyond the sun-kissed Highlands
    Of a new-found western world.

Thou hast heard the billows murmur
    In the dusky red man's ear,
That there is a Great, Great Spirit,
    Ever present, always near.

Thou hast seen red-handed rovers,
    Fierce and wild amid thy groves—
Ay, and buried wreckers' treasures
    On the margins of thy coves.

Well thou know'st the sailors' coming,
    Homeward-bound to kiss their brides,
Gladly singing in the morning
    As their vessels stemmed thy tides.

Youth and beauty rare have rested
    On thy gently swelling breast ;
Yachtsmen gay and weary seamen
    Love thy Horseshoe harbor rest.

Ah, what hearts of joys and sorrows
    Thou hast won in thy league's race !
Ah, what wealth of rich to-morrows
    Has flown seaward o'er thy face !

Ah, what throngs of ardent lovers
    Thou hast lost since days of yore !
Lost ! ah, yes ! Their spectre vessels
    Shall return to thee no more.

Fare thee well, thou generous river ;
　May life's current flow like thee,
Blessing lives and lands forever,
　And at last wind safe to sea !

RONDEAU—YE FRIENDLY BOOKS.

TO J. E. B.

YE friendly books—old friends of mine,
　There is no comradeship like thine ;
For who like thee canst always show
The wisdom which thy pages know,
Or who thy faithfulness divine ?
If we to thee our hearts incline,
Ready art thou with storied line
To banish all our grief and woe,
　　　　Ye friendly books.

Thou standest guard in rain or shine,
Like sentinels with gilded sign,
To point the way that all may know
The royal road to learning's show,
Where all mankind can delve or dine,
　　　　Ye friendly books.

A STOCKMAN'S ADVENTURES IN NEW YORK.

A STORY OF THE BUNCO GAME.

WHEN I give up trail-herdin', an' thought I 'd
    jes' vamoose,
An' see my nativ' kentry in a first-class freight
    caboose,
I wuz called er knowin' feller, an' I owned the
    Z Bar brand,
Fer in getherin' maverick yearlin's, I hed proved a
    lively hand.
I hed heerd thet New York city wuz a dandy
    place fer camps,
With water, grass, 'n clover—(pervided yer hed
    stamps).
So I riz a heap uv munney fer my pasture at " the
    Branch ";
An' got shet uv all my cattle thet wuz on the Z Bar
    Ranch ;
Then I bought a new sombrero, an' an outfit thet
    wuz neat,
An', sez I, "Wal neow, ole feller, we 'll get there
    with both feet."
So I rid to Jersey City, an' struck the round-ups
    there,
An' got aboard er steamer, an' took passage fer the
    fair ;

When at last the vessel landed I broke from her
    ole pen,
An' galloped 'cross a dirty trail uv teams an' cussin'
    men ;
An' up ole Cortlandt street I rolled, er-feelin' kinder
    blue,
When all ter onct, a feller cum an' sez, " Why, heow
    de do ?
I us'ter know yer in the West, yer name iz Joseph
    Breen ? "
" Yer wrong ! " sez I, " I 'm Texas riz, I cum from
    Abilene,
An' on the ole T diamond trail they calls me Jeeter
    Brown.
This hyar iz my furst takin' in uv this hyar takin'
    town ! "
" Oh, ah," he sez, " excuse me, sar ! I 'm wrong, I
    see—good-day."
An' then he vamoosed in the crowd, an' I hit big
    Broadway—
Huh ! thet 's a canyon fer yer ! with houses on each
    side,
An' the streams er-flowin' through hit iz a roarin'
    human tide ;
The Clear Fork of the Brazos, hit ain't nuthin', so I
    say,
Ter the noisy roarin' torrints wot 's a-flowin' through
    Broadway.
Oh, them crowds jes' kep' a-comin', allers rushin',
    hurryin' through,
An' there wuz thousands uv 'em, but nary one I knew.

Then I felt kinder home-sick fer my dugout in the
    vale,
Whar the ole owls wuz a-hooin' on the ole McKenzie
    Trail ;
Whar the cattle wuz a-browzin' on the yeller-blos-
    somed sod,
An' the pious plains wuz sleepin' with drowsy
    dreams uv God !
Oh, I longed fer them perairies in ole Texas far
    away,
Fer I felt like I wuz smotherin' on that suffercatin'
    day.
Wal, az I stood there a-studdyin', feelin' lonesum-
    like and down,
A hansum feller cum an' sed, "Why, how-dy !
    Jeeter Brown?
When did yer leave ole Texas ? Wot 's the news in
    Abilene ?
Heow iz Jim Lowden at the Bank, heow iz ole
    Keyrnal Deane?
I guess yer don't remember me, but I remembers
    you,
I 've often seen yer on the Range down by the
    Kickapoo.
I us'ter live in Abilene, my uncle 's Theo Heyck.
He 's sot me up in business hyar, my name iz
    Charles Van Slike."
Neow, you must jes' put up with me while stayin'
    hyar in town,
Fer I 'm powerful glad ter see yer, my ole friend,
    Jeeter Brown."

Wal, I commenced er-swellin', kinder tickled at
    sech talk,
From that hansum-lookin' feller on the Broadway
    uv New York ;
He knew my town's best people, an' hit 'peered
    like he knew me,
So I wuz glad ter see him, I wuz lonesum, don't
    yer see ?
Wal, Van he soon suggested thet we drink an'
    hev a chat
About our friends in Texas, an' ole times an' sech
    ez thet ;
So we mozied up the Bowery inter one uv them
    saloons
Whar the gals wuz slingin' whiskey an' a band wuz
    slingin' chunes.
Then we drank ter Editor Hoeny, we drank ter
    Keyrnal Deane,
An' we drank ter Sam Lapowski of the town of
    Abilene.
Oh, the likker flowed like water, huh, I tell yer,
    we wuz gay—
Oh, Van wuz jes' a daisy, an' I won't ferget that day.
When we left thet thar The-a-ter—an' went shyin'
    up the street,
I wuz feelin' powerful frisky — kinder skittish
    'round the feet.
Soon we cum to a Museum—whar they showed a
    hump-back horse,
An' Charley, he suggested thet we take hit in—uv
    course.

So we went inside sight-seein', till we met a chap
    who sed
He could tell us our char-ack-ters by a-feelin' uv
    our head ;
So we had our heads examined, most particularly
    mine,
Fer I wuz a splendid subjeck, full uv bumps, an'
    traits—an' wine.
Wal, after Doc hed lectured in er most delightful way,
He perlitely intermated thet he 'd like ter hev sum
    pay,
Then Charley showed a greenback, which the
    Doctor could n't change,
So, of course, I paid the charges, which appeared
    a little strange,
Fer the ole chap hed dun told us thet hiz lecture
    would be free,
But, since Van wuz in fer payin', why, so wuz I,
    yer see.
Right then I showed my money, the whole big
    chuffy pile,
Till Van commenced hiz smilin', and said that I 'd
    struck ile ;
Then he whispered confidential, sez he, " Now,
    Jeeter Brown,
You 'd better leave thet at the Bank afore you
    paint this town.
The city 's full uv sharpers, who are sure ter take
    you in,
So let 's go 'round to my cashyeer and hive away
    yer tin."

So we stepped "around the corner" to whar hiz
    Bank wuz at,
Whar we found a cashyeer writin', who wuz plez-
    zant-like an' fat.
Then I handed him my money, and took a big
    receipt,
An' after drinkin' tew the Bank, we started up the
    street.
The 'lectric lights wuz sizzin', fer hit wuz gittin' dark,
But we took them high-up steam-kyars, ter go to
    Central Park ;
An' we passed a beefy feller, full of New York
    Irish pride,
Who kep' up an awful yellin', "step lively there
    inside !"
But I soon lost my desires fer ter see the flyin'
    views,
Fer I wuz feelin' drowsy from thet Bowery Banker's
    Booze,
An' I never noticed Charley, may be so he wuz n't
    there.
Fer I fell asleep a-rockin', an' a-rushin' through
    the air.
But hit hain't no us' ter finish, the sequil 's kinder
    tame,
Fer yer see, I wuz the victum uv thet little Bunco
    Game.
Slick Charley an' hiz pardners—the man on Cort-
    landt Street,
That cashyeer an' thet Doctor, hed done me up
    complete.

Though I got my ole six-shooter, an' caved an'
    charged around
A-lookin' fer my munney, them chaps could not be
    found.
Ah, them Bunco Boys iz artful, az all pious men
    agree,
If yer ever run across 'em, jes' round 'em up—fer
    me !
An' when yer social fellers leaves the home-range
    with yer chork,
Jest remember my experiunce with them sharpers
    in New York.

———

TO A LADY PLAYING THE GUITAR.

L. S.

A S I pensive sit and listen, while her jewelled
    fingers glisten
  Through some tuneful old romanza, on her airy
    sad guitar ;
I indulge in recollections, and fond dreams of old
    affections,
  Which haunt my vagrant fancy like a vision
    from afar.

Ah, I hear her spirit straying o'er the strings she 's
    softly playing,
  And I feel a gentle rapture swelling through this
    heart of mine ;

Far beyond the music stealing there 's a hidden
  chord of feeling,
 Which woos my restless nature like some melody
  divine.

Yes, my lady proud and queenly, playing there
  midst dreams serenely,
 That tender chord has bound me to the portals
  of thy heart.
There, ah there, O let me hover, for I fain would
  be your lover,
 Who from thy tuneful presence wouldst never-
  more depart.

THE VIKINGS OF CAPE ANN.

YE fishermen of Gloucester,
   That sail the Northern Sea,
Ye hardy sons of Neptune,
   All hail, I say, to thee !
Though history sings of Norsemen,
   And Scotland boasts her clan,
Here 's to our Yankee skippers,
   The Vikings of Cape Ann.

Ye nurslings of the billows
   That wail on Norman's woe,
There were no better seamen
   In days of long ago ;

Through storms and death and danger,
　Through dark, wild winter nights,
They cruise the seas from Iceland,
　To Thatcher's Island lights.

Nursed by the wild Nor'easter,
　And cradled by the sea,
These rugged Northern sailors
　Are stalwart, bold, and free.
Through fogs and blinding snowstorms,
　From Labrador to Maine,
They ply their dangerous calling
　With hook and trawl and seine.

How oft at early morning,
　'Midst dreams of summer's calm,
I 've watched their vessels sailing
　Seaward from Annisquam.
And oft when twilight's kisses
　Have made the ocean smile,
I 've seen their dories dancing
　Off wild Monhegan's Isle.

No matter where you find them,
　Where e'er these vessels be,
They breathe a tale of danger,
　A romance of the sea ;
They hint of wrecks and hardship,
　Of toil-worn, active lives,
Of tempest-tossed, doomed seamen,
　Of sad-eyed, wistful wives.

THE VIKINGS OF CAPE ANN.

For many a family circle,
　　On bold New England's main
Waits for some sea-gone member,
　　But waits, alas, in vain.
And many a tangled graveyard
　　Along that billowed lea,
Contains this sad old story,
　　This legend—" Lost at Sea."

And yet these true-born sailors,
　　In spite of dangerous toil,
Still love their restless ocean
　　And scorn the steady soil.
Let history sing of Norsemen,
　　And Scotland praise her clan,
Here 's to our Yankee skippers,
　　The Vikings of Cape Ann.

East Gloucester, Mass., 1892.

TO SUMMER.

A SONNET.

DECKED with her roses, roses rare,
　　With drowsy dreams in her laughing eyes,
The Summer drifts from the Southern skies,
While wreathed in her warm, glad golden hair ;
The sunbeams glow like jewels there,
　　And borne afar on her perfumed sighs
　　The choired songs of the birds arise,
Through the soft, voluptuous, vibrant air.
　　Lo ! the slumbering lilies breathe and swoon,

With pale delight, for the Summer's voice
   Has wed fair May to a royal June,
And the bridesmaid Earth has blessed the choice,
   For the echoes ring with a joyous tune
Which bids all listening life rejoice.

TEXAS TYPES—"THE BAD MAN."

H E has a drooping winged moustache,
   A little chin goatee ;
His face is hard, he dresses flash,
   His eyes are strange to see.

His boots have two-inch concave heels,
   He wears a big slouch hat ;
He 's full of *sand!* he never squeals,
   Has too much nerve for that.

Oh, yes, he gambles—*on the square*—
   He sports gay diamond pins ;
He has that cool, dare-devil air
   Whereby the gambler wins.

You 'll always find "he 's killed his man "
   Or "rounded up a band,"
Or slain some greaser Mexican
   Down on the Rio Grande.

And yet with all his scars and sin
   He seldom seeks a fight,

But when he does, he shoots to win
   Against all odds in sight.

You 'll find him in the larger towns,
   He haunts the big bar-rooms,
And, ah ! He haunts those silent mounds
   Which mark the city's tombs.

For like some flowers of colder climes,
   Which wither while yet green,
This Texas type of frosty times
   Soon leaves life's thorny scene.

For he is now beyond the age
   And order rules the day ;
Texas has passed the pistol stage,
   The law has come to stay.

TO THE MEMORY OF GEN. R. S. MAC-
KENZIE.

(Border hero, Indian fighter, and graduate of West Point, General in United States Army stationed in San Antonio, Texas. " He died of mental troubles " at New York, in 1889.)

MACKENZIE, thy warfare is o'er—
   Thy bold, loyal heart is at rest,
Thy noble soul suffers earth's sorrows no more,
For thy bark sailing seaward has reached the lone
     shore
  Of that far-away land of the blest.

Brave hero, we mourn not for thee,
   Thou hast gone from life's troubles and care ;
Thy stern soldier spirit forever is free ;
It has joined the Grand Army encamped by the
     sea
   In the bivouac realms over there !

And yet since by love thou wert slain,
   In pity we bow o'er thy bier,
And we sigh when we think of thy story of pain,
Of that proud, loyal love that thou lavished in
     vain,
   And in secret we shed the sad tear.

But we feel that affection like thine
   Is not lost 'neath the gloom of the sod,
That beyond the dark valley where love is divine,
It will glow evermore and eternally shine
   In the balm-breathing Edens of God.

Mackenzie, true soldier, good-by ;
   The wind wails thy long reveille,
And to-night on the plains where the weird cay-
    otes cry,
Far away o'er thy trail 'neath the tents of the sky,
   I breathe this slight tribute to thee.

THE FLORIDA KEYS.

FAR away in the land of the graceful palmetto,
  Where the shy Southern Cross woos the fair
    crescent moon ;
Where the mocking-birds sing midst the mangoes
    and myrtle,
  And life is a dream of perennial June ;
Where the nautilus floats o'er an ocean of azure,
  And the rarest of incense perfumes every breeze ;
There, there far away are some tropical islands,
  Fair islands of beauty—the Florida Keys.

There the lime-tree and orange forever are wooing
  And showering gifts to the passionate rose,
There the spectre crane dreams 'neath the droop-
    ing banana,
    And the warm, vibrant air breathes the life of
    repose ;
There the frigate-bird drifts like a dream in the
    heavens,
    While the pelican broods on the mango-bush
    near,
There the silver king swims through a palace of
    coral
    'Midst gardens of sponges that bloom all the
    year.

There the lonely loon calls to the fair snowy ibis
  While the Seminole paddles his lazy canoe ;

There the cocoanut grows and the guava is bloom-
    ing
  Beneath a soft sky of cerulean hue ;
Oh, the color and light and the charm of these
    islands,
  These islands of coral 'midst emerald seas,
There the tired heart blooms into garlands of
    fancy,
  Ah, life is divine on the Florida Keys.
BISCAYNE BAY, Fla.

TEXAS TYPES, " THE TENDERFOOT."

YOU can tell him by his " weepons !"
    And his soft, confiding air,
His bran-new gorgeous outfit,
    And his high-priced aged mare.

He is primed with tales of dangers
    In the wild and woolly West,
And bold dreams of robber rangers
    Disturb his nightly rest.

He has queer ideas of Texas ;
    Thinks her people live in gore !
He seems queer to all the sexes,
    For his actions make folks roar.

But he soon gets used to chaff, sir,
    For he 's green as April wheat,
Yet for men to make you laugh, sir,
    I commend the Tenderfeet.

"FAR AWAY IN THE LAND OF THE GRACEFUL PALMETTO."

Soon he pines to be a cowboy
　And to ride a pitching horse,
Ah, then you ought to see him.
　For he 's paralyzed—of course.

Then he writes some lying story
　To his family far away,
Some brave tale of border glory
　Where he figures in the play.

If he goes back where he came from,
　He assumes a Western air,
Then I tell you he is woolly !
　And his actions make folks stare.

Yes, you know I tell the truth, sir,
　Now I never lie for pelf,
But I was—yes ! in my youth, sir,
　Was a Tenderfoot myself ! !

BROADWAY, N. Y., 6 P. M.

A LONE in the crowded thoroughfare
　　In the whirlpool of Broadway,
I wander on in the evening air
And watch the storied faces there
　At the close of the busy day.

On, on they rush with joy and woe,
　Each hurrying past his neighbor ;
The rich, the poor, the high and low,

Like a restless tide they ebb and flow
From the rugged shores of labor.

There are faces there in that motley crowd
Which show misfortune's fingers ;
There are some with features cold and proud,
And some with shame and sorrow bowed,
And some where pleasure lingers.

On, on they sweep with rush and roar,
A breathing stream of motion ;
With wrecks and driftwood on its shore,
A river flowing evermore
Towards dim oblivion's ocean.

And yet that whirl of hope and fear,
That torrent of endeavor,
Shall ebb and flow year after year,
For though life's bubbles disappear,
Its tide swells on forever.

REFLECTIONS AT A YOUNG LADIES' TEA PARTY.

THERE 'S a beautiful home in a realm that I
know
In the proud mountain town of Montclair,
Where the robins are singing and the wild asters
grow,
Where the warm zephyrs play and the sun loves to
glow,
Round a mansion which love builded there.

And there by a mountain which dreams of the sea,
   One autumnal rare afternoon,
As the soft twilight shadows stole down o'er the lea,
I attended a party—A Five o'Clock Tea—
   A party I won't forget soon.

Oh, the laughter and joy of those glad golden
     hours
   Ah, the beauty I saw gathered there
Was as lovely and pure as a bouquet of flowers,
It was culled from the gardens of youth's royal
     bowers
   That bloom in that Eden—Montclair.

As the music arose with its plaintive bassoon,
   And the sunset's gold arrows were cast,
There swept through my soul on that fair after-
     noon
Old memories as fragrant as roses of June,
   Old far-away dreams of the past.

As I watched the leaf curtains expand with the
     breeze,
   And saw those fair maidens drift by,
I thought of old days by the far azure seas,
Of an old hacienda 'neath magnolia trees'
   Of a home 'neath the tropical sky ;

Of a home where the cypress is shrouded with
     moss,
   Where the jasmine breathes forth its perfume ;

In a land far away 'neath the fair Southern Cross,
Where the lilies and roses are drooping with loss
  By the side of a lone tangled tomb.

Ah, then as I looked at that beautiful throng
  Of loveliness, laughter, and youth,
There swelled through my heart like the sigh of a
      song
An echo of sorrow, a whisper of wrong,
  A question of Nature's stern truth.

Oh, why must love's lilies soon learn of life's frost,
  Oh, why must youth's beauties soon fade ;
Like the leaves in yon forest, soon, soon tempest-
    tossed,
They must wither and perish and forever be lost
  In the gloom of oblivion's shade.

Ah, this question of life and its wierd mystery—
  Soon, soon the last bugle will call,
Soon the muffled drum sounds the long, lone re-
    veille,
And the spectre ships sail o'er death's desolate sea
  And *Hic Jacet* soon answers for all.

  Ah, yes, as I looked at that festival throng,
  Of beauty and youth gathered there,
There swept through my soul, like the sigh of a
    song,
An echo of sorrow which did not belong
  To that Five o'Clock Tea in Montclair.

FAREWELL, FAREWELL, MY LADY.

FAREWELL, farewell my lady.   The mourn-
ful zephyrs sigh
That summer days are over, that we must say
good-by,
For all the drooping roses have felt that wistful
spell
Which haunts the listening landscape when sum-
mer sighs " farewell."   .
The sea-birds' songs are weary, and weary seems
the sea,
For mists of separation have parted you and me.
No more we walk together along the lonely shore ;
The lanes, the rocks, the meadows, remember us
no more.
Alas, the season 's over, and you will soon forget
Your scattered summer lovers, who left you with
regret.

For now you 're in the city engulfed in fashion's
cares,
And flirting with your lovers among the million-
aires;
Your costumes are bewitching, you 're at the opera
seen,
And though a slave to fashion, you still are
beauty's queen.
You visit all the theatres, you dabble in the arts,

You ride out in your carriage, you trample over
    hearts,
You go to church, my lady—I long to see you
    there,
To view that glimpse of heaven, my angel bowed
    in prayer.
But no, I 'm distant from you, and you, ah, you
    forget
Your absent summer lovers, who dream about you
    yet.

But, ah, proud pensive lady, sometimes perhaps
    there 'll be
A far-off recollection, a longing for the sea ;
Sometimes within your chamber, beside the em-
    bers' glow,
Perhaps your jaded fancies will sigh for long ago ;
Perchance your weary nature will dream of sum-
    mer's calm,
Those peaceful woods and meadows, that vine em-
    bowered farm ;
Then when you 're tired of fashion and all its glit-
    tering cares,
And tired of flirting lovers and doubtful million-
    aires,
Ah, then, ah, then, my lady, perhaps you 'll not
    forget
One loyal summer lover who 's faithful to you yet.

AL FRESCO !

A ROMANTIC youth of Bar Harbor so fair
    Was madly in love with a maid,
And once after dark in the cool evening air
    He attempted a sly serenade.

He warbled and sang with his rare tenor voice
    Till morning bejewelled the skies,
But, alas for youth's hopes ! the maid of his choice
    Never came in response to his sighs.

At last tired out and weary at heart,
    And swelling with rage and regret,
He went to her door, where he read, with a start,
    " This large vacant house is—To Let ! "

————

TO THE MEMORY OF MAJOR DANIEL GANO.

BORN, 1794 ; DIED, 1873.

H IS life was a poem of kindness and grace,
    A sermon of love for mankind,
His hope, like the sun, illumined life's face,
He was good to the poor—he exalted his race,
    He was noble, sincere, and refined !
12

His friends they were many—his equals were
  few,
 .He was cultured and courtly and cool,
He was gracious and generous to all whom he
  knew,
He was gallant and fearless, an American true,
  "A gentleman of the old school."

His monument 's more than all marble that 's
  scrolled,
  For his memory surpasses the arts ;
By the chisels of Love his virtues are told,
And his name is emblazoned in letters of gold
  On the portals of all of our hearts.

TO A DALLAS LADY.

I SING this song to one who long
  Has charmed me with a spell ;
A lady who has blessed my life
  Far more than I can tell.
'T were vain to try, I cannot guage,
  Her charms in feeble measures,
For, oh, her mind and soul refined
  Are rich in mental treasures.

Her song, with smiles, all care beguiles,
  To her the pow'r is given
To gild all weary hearts with joy,
  And make this earth a heaven.

"A GENTLEMAN OF THE OLD SCHOOL."
(MAJOR DANIEL GANO.)

She is a garland of delight,
  A queen of royal manner,
A wreath of flowers from Southern bowers,
  From fair Louisiana.

Ah, yes ! she 's kind, you 'll always find
  Her heart is free from malice,
She seems ideal, but yet she 's real,
  This lady lives in Dallas.
This song I send to her, my friend,
  The loveliest of the sexes,
Long may she live to bless the world
  And reign a Queen of Texas.

————

THE LONELY CONGAREE.

LONG ago in South Carolina,
  Near fair Charleston by the sea,
Stood a lovely old plantation
  On the lazy Congaree.

There in drooping Southern splendor
  Waved the tall palmetto trees,
There the fragrant, rare magnolia
  Breathed its blessings to the breeze.

There the sunlight loved to linger
  Through the golden incensed hours,
There the humming-birds were wooing
  In a wilderness of flowers.

Ah, what memories of enchantment
  Doth my wayward fancy see,
When I think of that old homestead
  On the dreaming Congaree.

Here to-night within my chamber,
  Pensive by the embers' glow,
How my memory backward wanders
  To the realms of long ago.

I can hear the darkies singing,
  And the drowsy hum of bees,
And the laughter of the children
  Playing 'neath the cypress trees.

On the airy, bowered veranda,
  Partly hidden from the sight,
I can see a graceful hammock
  And a vision clad in white.

'T is the vision of a lady,
  Proud and pensive, darkly fair,
Fairer than the royal flowers
  That were swooning in her hair.

Ah, that face of wistful beauty,
  And those pure, commanding eyes
Told of noble aspirations
  And the dreams of Paradise.

There my roving, restless spirit
  Found at last a resting-place ;

"AH, THAT FACE OF WISTFUL BEAUTY."

There I found my earthly Eden
    In the heaven of a face.

Then my life was filled with music
    And my heart from care was free,
For I loved that dark-eyed lady
    Of the dear old Congaree.

There we floated on the river
    In a lazy-oared canoe,
There we dreamed life's old, old story,
    Old indeed, yet always new.

How those moonbeams danced and glistened
    Through the soft, voluptuous air,
How the ripples paused and listened
    To the romance whispered there.

How the zephyrs breathed their passion
    As they kissed each truant tress,
How those drooping lashes quivered
    When she softly answered "yes !"

.   .   .   .   .

But, alas for youth's fair visions,
    That fond dream was not to be,
For she sleeps below the lilies
    By the *sobbing* Congaree.

Yes, the mournful winds are wailing
    Through those sombre cypress trees,
And the flowers weep with sorrow,
    'Midst the sighings of the bees.

Though that river still flows seaward
   As it flowed in days of yore,
It is haunted now forever
   With that spectre—*nevermore !*

Yes, to-night I 'm sad and weary,
   Pensive by the embers' glow,
For my spirit, like the river,
   Fondly dreams of long ago.

Ah, my haunted soul drifts backward
   Through the realms of memory,
For my heart is with the lilies
   By the lonely Congaree.

———

THE SQUALL—OFF SANDY HOOK, N. J.

HIGH o'er the bowsprit flies the brine,
   As we cleave the crests of the white-cap sea ;
Once more we quaff of the ocean's wine,
   Once more our prisoner hearts are free.
With mainsail reefed and helm hard down,
   With rails a swash and a bending boom,
Our stanch sloop reels past the bell buoy brown
   And shivers and leaps through the gathering
      gloom.

With the wild wind's song in the whistling shrouds
   And a seething sea in our frosty wake,
We scan the scurrying, muttering clouds
   And grimly note each tack we make.

On the leeward bow is Sandy Hook ;
  To the windward far the waves are white ;
In the lap of night the Highlands look
  Like some huge sea-snake with eyes of light.

The hissing rain is loosed at last—
  It sweeps and swishes around us all—
The cordage wails, and the groaning mast
  Bends far to the kiss of a nor'east squall.
We roll and pitch through the angry sea,
  O'er hills and valleys of waves we fly,
Till the hoarse, long order of " H-a-r-d a-lee ! "
  Is lost in the answers of " Aye, aye, aye ! "

With rattle and roar we go about,
  The shivering sails swell out afar,
With wind astern and our boom far out
  We weather and pass the harbor bar.
The anchor lights shine out and gleam
  Like dancing jewels in night's dark crown,
While across the bay twin beacons beam
  And glow o'er the Navesink Highland town.

Now the storm has ceased, and the wind has passed,
  Yet a wild sea wails on the windward shore ;
With all things tight, and our anchor cast,
  The yachtsman's cruise for the day is o'er.
Eight bells have struck as we go below
  To enjoy our cabin of snug delight,
But we soon turn in, for a lullaby slow
  Chugs under our keel—Good-night ! Good-
    night !

Sloop Yacht " *Myrtis.*" Summer, 1892.

FAREWELL.

FAREWELL, farewell, ye summer flowers,
   Pale autumn cries, prepare !
Adieu, adieu, ye fragrant bowers,
Death lingers near with leafy showers
   To deck thy funeral bier !

Alas, alas, youth's flowers of yore,
   Oh, where, oh, where are ye ?
Dead, sigh the zephyrs to the shore ;
Lost, sob the echoes evermore ;
   Gone, wails the whispering sea.

Good-by, good-by, since we must go,
   Since all must hear Death's knell.
Adieu, ye withered wreaths of woe ;
Adieu, stern Nature's echoes low,
   Life is a long Farewell !

———

"OUTWARD BOUND."

Steamer *Concho en route* north.
GALVESTON, June, 1892.

PROUD Southern land, farewell, farewell !
   Our bark is on the sea ;
The anchor 's weighed, the breezes swell—
The *Concho* sobs its parting knell
   To bear us far from thee.

The warm gulf zephyrs woo the shrouds
　　With many a wistful sigh ;
The ocean's dome is flecked with clouds
And from the seaward gazing crowds
　　There swells—a long good-by.

The whispering ripples onward glide
　　With loving, laughing sound.
Our stately vessel breasts the tide
And filled with steamer breathing pride
　　She plunges " Outward Bound ! "

Though far on foreign shores we dream
　　Or 'midst the isles of Maine,
Fond memories of the South will gleam
And fancy's inward eye will beam
　　With thoughts of—home again !

Soon sinks the sun in twilight's sky ;
　　Sad wanes the wistful light,
The eager sea-birds homeward hie,
Like wingèd dreams that landward fly
　　Fair Southern land—good-night !

A QUESTION OF PROFIT.

WHEN the curtain rolls down, and thy life's
　　　farce is ended,
And the grim prompter, Death, calls an end to
　　　your part,

Will it profit you then that your life was expended
  In hoarding and stinting while starving your
    heart?

When the story is told and thy book has been
    written,
  And the contents show nothing but chapters on
    self,
Will it profit you then that you 're gone and for-
    gotten,
  And lost in oblivion and laid on the shelf?

When the last debt of all has been surely collected
  And you sleep in the silence and gloom 'neath
    the sod,
Will it profit you then, when your life is dissected,
  And your shams and your cheats are computed
    by God?

THE DYING SCOUT.

A STORY OF THE ABILENE COUNTRY, TEXAS.

COME, Pinto, ole feller, creep close to me side,
  For the norther is comin' across the Divide;
I knows its wild muzic, so shrill an' so strange,
An' the owls iz a-hoo-in' outside on the range;
The cayotes ar' roamin' the prairies ter-night,
They 're awaitin' fer me, they 're hungry with fight.
This pain it ar' awful, an' the meat iz all gone,
An' the fire won't last, I 'm afeered, till the morn,

An' our blanket iz ragged, but we iz alone,
So we 'll share it ter-night, though I 'm cold az a
    stone ;
But them flames iz a-laughin' an' smilin' with glow,
An' they make me feel good like in days long ago,
When I wuz light-hearted an' waz n't a fool,
An' played mumblepeg on the grass, near the
    school,
With dear little Bess—bless her honest blue eyes—
But she 's far away, mabbie home in the skies.
Fer thet thar Jim Basset, the storekeeper's son,
He jilted my Bessie an' thought it whar fun,—
An' he ruined her, too, so I settled him ;
(P'r'aps I would n't be hyar if it waz n't fer Jim)
Oh, Bessie wuz lovely, all kindness an' joy,
An' I jist worshipped her with the love uv a boy.

   .   .   .   .   .

But, Pinto, ole feller, thet mother er mine,
Wuz the darlin'est mother, jes' angel divine,
She 'd nurs' the sick nabors, wharever they 'd be
An' she allers wuz prayin' fer Sandy an' me ;
But Sandy fergits her, an' its little he keers
Fer his brother thet 's scoutin' for nigh twenty years.
Then thar wuz Aunt Lucy, so gentle and mild,
She allers wuz smilin' an' said I " wuz wild " ;
Yet somehow she liked me, it whar no mistake,
Fer she allers wuz givin' me soft ginger cake ;
An' she 'd tell me long stories an' sing ter me too,
Oh, I tell yer I loved her, I loved me Aunt Lou.
Her heart it wuz bigger than the warm tropic sea,

An' sich lives ar' sermons, ter fellers like me,
Who b'lieves in religion thet comes from the heart,
An' hates false pretence, an' the hippercrit's part.
I jedge a man's actions, instead uv his pray'r,
An' I never goes back on what 's honest an' squar',
An' though I 'm so triflin,' such a poor human clod,
Wild nature hez taught me the wizdom uv God.
An' some day, ole feller, when I 'm over this pain,
We 'll go home tergether, an' be happy again.

.   .   .   .   .   .

We 'll find the old homestid, with its birds an' its
    trees,
Whar life wuz all music an' flowers an' bees ;
Whar I loved ter go swimmin' with the lilies so
    cool,
In them years long er go when I hated the school.
But the fire is dyin', its dark an' so cold,
An' Pinto, ole feller, I 'm puny an' old ;
An' the door iz a-creaking so sad in the wind,
But we 's close tergether, ole chap, never mind.
Hez I ever hurt yer sence I found yer thet day,
A perp on the trail an' the boys far away ?
Yer knows what I 'm sayin', I see by yer eyes,
But yer mad, my ole doggie, an' thet 's a surprize.
Thar ! thar ! my ole feller, what 's makin' yer bark ?
I did n't serpose yer wuz skeered uv the dark ;
But yer say them iz eyes gleamin' in at the door,
Wall, I never have noticed sich doin's before.
So Pinto, good feller, creep close to me side,
Fer the norther is moanin' across the Divide.

Hark! muzic! I heers it, so mournful an' strange,
Like lost children's wailin' outside on the range ;
But the cayotes are watchin' our dugout ter-night,
They 're waitin' fer me, an' they 're hungry with
  fight ;
An' I am so puny, an' so shiverin' too,
But Pinto, dear feller, I 'm pardners with you ;
An' you are so honest an' faithful an' brave,
Thet you 'd starve ter death on your ole marster's
  grave ;
But I feels better now than fer many a day,
So cheer up, ole feller, don't whine that 'er way ;
Fer when the perairies iz kivered with flowers,
An' the mockin'-birds sing an' the hills iz all ours,
We 'll hunt an' we 'll roam az we did long er go,
Two pardners tergether, in pleasure an' woe ;
An' we 'll go home agin, to the banks of the stream,
Whar the ole folks iz livin' an' life iz a dream ;
An' with all our wrong-doin's we 'll try ter live
  right ;
An', Pinto, dear feller—old Pinto !—good-night !

But Pinto, poor fellow, moans wild at his side,
For the scout, with the norther, has crossed the
  Divide.

THE END.

Printed in the USA
CPSIA information can be obtained
at www.ICGtesting.com
LVHW021111281223
767380LV00077B/104

9 781016 182980